Teaching About Language in the

ONE WEEK

D0537212

Second Edition

Rebecca Bunting

David Fulton Publishers
London

Published in association with the University of Surrey Roehampton

David Fulton Publishers Ltd
The Chiswick Centre, 414 Chiswick High Road, London W4 5TF
www.fultonpublishers.co.uk

First published in Great Britain in 1997 by David Fulton Publishers

Note: The rights of Rebecca Bunting to be identified as the authors of this work
have been asserted by them in accordance with the Copyright, Designs and
Patents Act 1988.

David Fulton Publishers is a division of Granada Learning Limited, part of
Granada plc.

British Library Cataloguing in Publication Data
A catalogue record for this book is available from the British Library.

ISBN 1-85346-667-0

Typeset by FiSH Books, London
Printed and bound in Great Britain

Contents

Preface

This book is for teachers and student teachers who are interested in language, in children's understanding of language and in the teacher's role in developing children's knowledge about language.

It suggests activities for the primary classroom which help children to look at language, at how it is used and how it works. It contextualises the approaches underpinning these activities so that their intentions and purposes are made clear.

The book is a contribution to the ongoing and controversial debate about what children need to know about language, a debate which gained momentum in the 1980s and which has since been shaped and driven by government reports on English teaching, successive versions of the National Curriculum for English and, more recently, the National Literacy Strategy (NLS). In addition, many of the linguistic terms and concepts discussed here in an educational context are current requirements in relation to teachers' knowledge and understanding of the subject of English.

Many of the students and teachers I meet professionally feel that they have very little knowledge about language, although they invariably know more than they realise. The requirements for the award of qualified teacher status, as specified in DfEE Circular 4/98, set challenging targets for knowledge about language. The teaching of grammar causes most anxiety and it is this issue which usually grabs the headlines when English teaching is in the news. Understanding about the grammatical forms of English is an important aspect of language knowledge, but it is not the only one and not the most important one. This book discusses the arguments about teaching grammar and places this aspect of knowledge about language in a primary years framework, particularly the later primary years when, on the whole, children are operating more independently in language. This wider framework involves a recognition of the functions of language and the importance of context.

Debates about what to teach children about language may sometimes seem more relevant to secondary school than to primary, particularly when grammar is seen as the only knowledge about language worth having. It has been argued that children in the primary years should not be encumbered by the need to learn about language, because they have yet to gain full control over reading and writing, and competence must precede reflection. However, I would argue that learning to use language and learning about language are not separate processes but are integrated and interrelated. Teachers and children need to engage in regular discussions about language, so that the children develop a questioning attitude to language and see talking about language as relevant and interesting. The NLS now brings this issue into sharp focus.

It is in the primary years that children's interest in and awareness of language can be most readily fostered. Learning about language gives children the analytical tools with which to test, judge, critique and question the language they encounter, so that they can understand how it is used, its meanings and intentions. To do this, children will need some terminology for talking about, describing and explaining aspects of language; the knowledge and enthusiasm of the teacher will be crucial in creating appropriate contexts through which such learning can come about.

In this way, a rich culture of talk about language will be created. Talking about language will become a normal and regular part of classroom life, not an exception and certainly not limited or constrained to brief timetabled slots in the curriculum.

This second edition makes selective reference to the requirements of the NLS, which was implemented in primary schools in England and Wales in September 1998. At the time of writing, plans are being drawn up to extend the strategy into the early years of secondary education. The document governing these literacy developments, the Framework for Teaching, lists what children must be taught in each term of their primary schooling, including the Reception year. It establishes a pedagogy for teaching which is unprecedented in our educational history.

These requirements will be considered in terms of what the NLS says about teaching about language – that is, what children are expected to know about language, not simply their implicit competence in using language which is the strategy's prime purpose.

This book is in two parts. Part One, Language, Language Education and Linguistics, proposes a model for learning about language. Part Two, Language Activities, suggests a wide range of approaches to developing children's understandings about language.

The Glossary contains brief explanations of key linguistic terms. These are in **bold** throughout the text where fuller explanations of some of them may be found.

Rebecca Bunting
Chelmsford
August 2000

Acknowledgements

Acknowledgement is made to the following for permission to use copyright material:

'Ten Tall Oaktrees', from *A Mouse in my Roof* by Richard Edwards, first published in the UK by Orchard Books, a division of the Watts Publishing Group, 96 Leonard Street, London EC2A 4RH; the folk tale, 'The Baker's Daughter', from *Clever Gretchen and Other Forgotten Folktales* by Alison Lurie, a scrambled version of which is reproduced by permission of Reed Consumer Books, London and The Melanie Jackson Agency, New York; 'The Writer of this Poem' by Roger McGough, reproduced by permission of Peters Fraser and Dunlop Group Ltd on behalf of Roger McGough; two short extracts from *George's Marvellous Medicine* by Roald Dahl, published by Cape, reproduced by permission of David Higham Associates on behalf of the author's estate.

PART 1
Language, Language Education and Linguistics

Chapter 1
Principles of language study

A LITTLE HISTORY

Two negatives make a positive, so you must never say *I didn't do nothing*. Never start a sentence with *and* or *but*, or finish one with a preposition. There is no such word as *ain't*.

This is me talking to my class when I first began teaching English. I made these pronouncements, and many just like them, with the best of intentions – I wanted the children to do well and progress in English, and particularly in their writing. I wanted to help them to understand some of the conventions and to ensure that they used grammatically correct forms in their written work. I recognised that even though these were conventions of changing usage and not laws cast in stone for all time, conventions do come to be seen as rules and I felt that, since people conformed to these rules, I had to ensure that the children could understand them and use them, so that they would become proficient language users. We did some exercises designed to improve specific aspects of their writing. They learned how to identify main and subordinate clauses, and they happily filled in gaps and spotted grammatical mistakes in passages I gave them.

I knew these rules because I myself had been taught them at school and now it was my turn to pass them on. I believed that this was what English teachers were supposed to do. Somewhere there existed accepted standards of written and spoken language, and I expected my class to aspire to and achieve those standards. I believed my role was to keep out all corrupting influences (such as the way they spoke at home), to correct the incorrect and make perfect the imperfect. Although at that point I had not read the Newbolt Report, *The Teaching of English in England* (HMSO 1921), or even heard of it actually, my attitudes and approaches are signalled there:

The great difficulty of teachers in elementary schools in many districts is that they have to fight against the powerful influences of evil habits of speech contracted in home and street. (p. 59)

Children's language experiences and expertise from outside school were considered to be dangerous and to impede what schools were trying to do. The language children brought into school from home was seen as a dirty habit, as debased and evil. The teacher's role was to compensate for these bad influences from home. The use of the word 'evil' and the sense of moral opprobrium in this quotation is shocking to us today.

We can compare this with a quotation from a very influential report published 54 years later, *A Language for Life*, known as the Bullock Report (DES 1975), initially commissioned by the then Secretary of State, Margaret Thatcher, to advise on the teaching of reading, but actually including all aspects of language development in its remit. Here we can see a change in attitude to the language children bring to school and to the status of non-standard dialects of English.

> No child should be expected to cast off the language and culture of the home as he [sic] crosses the school threshold and the curriculum should reflect these aspects of his life. (para 20.5)

Although it was referring to the needs of what were called 'overseas' children, the report marked the beginnings of a recognition of the value of every child's home culture. We can trace the influence of such beliefs in the report of the National Curriculum English Working Group, *English For Ages 5–16*, (DES 1989) known as the Cox Report, where there is a clear recognition of the political complexities of this educational issue and the potential psychological trauma for children who are made to change the way they speak. As Cox (1991) later argued:

> Teaching Standard English demands great sensitivity from the teacher. It is dangerous to tell a 5-year-old girl or boy that his or her mother uses language incorrectly. Adolescents are going to be embarrassed and ashamed if a teacher suggests that their dialect, which is part of their identity, must be radically changed. (p. 33)

Although the authors of both the Bullock and the Cox reports demonstrate greater sensitivity to the needs of the child and to the political and cultural implications of outlawing the child's natural speech than was evident in 1921, the extent to which these reports influenced the attitudes of parents, politicians and others outside the teaching profession is open to question. The belief that non-standard English equates with *bad* English has prevailed and the best efforts of linguists and teachers have not significantly changed public attitudes. As a beginning teacher, I didn't blame the children for not being able to write as well as I wanted them to. I approached my teaching and marking with missionary zeal, repelling a split infinitive (Star Trek was only just establishing its cult status, so the split infinitive had not really come to people's attention: one was yet to boldly go anywhere) and fending off a 'lend/borrow' or a 'teach/learn' mistake with my trusty bible, the dictionary.

My purpose was to teach the children *explicitly* about the forms of written Standard English so that they would use this knowledge to improve their writing *skills*. I wanted to teach them how to use language, what was allowed and what forbidden. I was acting as editor of all their work, making it better. I was also trying to give the children, at least minimally, a language for talking about language – **metalanguage**. This involved teaching them the names of the parts of speech and I would try to enliven this by playing 'spot the adverb' in a poem, or 'underline all the prepositions'. Using their mental checklist in English tests and examinations, the children would write 'There are no adverbs of time in this passage' and I would feel a glow of pride.

I did come to realise that I didn't know enough about whether there was a relationship between knowing about language and being able to use it appropriately and effectively. I also realised that spoken language and written language, though sharing many similarities, differ grammatically; that there is a complex relationship between spoken language and written language; and that I was not accounting for this. Did children actually write as they spoke, as so many people seemed to be arguing at the time? Well, yes and no. How could I talk about this with the children? What was my role here? Did knowledge of grammar apply only to writing or was there a connection with reading? Was knowledge about grammar all there was to know about language? And (never start a sentence with 'and') most significantly, I realised that all my proscribing of their language was not encouraging the children in their development as writers: if anything I was impeding their creativity and skill. I watched as they rubbed holes in their paper in an effort to get something right and ended up writing hardly anything at all. How could I deal with this? Teaching children about language was an uphill struggle.

This brief autobiographical vignette comes not from the 1950s as you might have thought but from the early 1980s. I don't think it is unusual or exceptional. I was taking my place in a tradition of English-language teaching which had a long history, largely because I did not know any other way. What I knew most about was not linguistics but literature, because I had studied that at university. I was not well-equipped to teach language.

I doubt that many children developed a lasting interest in language as a result of my teaching, though many of them would carry the rules uncritically around with them and no doubt pass them on to their own children. When I look back on my language teaching I see myself as a fond Mrs Chips, graciously smiling, a tear in my eye, on all the generations of children who had come under my influence. Or perhaps it was more like Chinese whispers, with the message becoming more and more mangled?

LAY AND PROFESSIONAL PERSPECTIVES: THE GREAT GRAMMAR DEBATE

In my teaching of English I treated language as a fixed system with rules to be learned and applied. I focused on the forms of language, usually the written forms, and on standard written English. I assumed that if children learned certain rules, they would become better users of language. I assumed that without this explicit knowledge, there could be no real fluency or quality of expression in writing. In other words, I took for granted that to be competent, you need to know first how the thing (language) works, that to know how it works and to make it work requires a knowledge of the internal mechanisms, in this case the grammar of the English language. This is a belief often uncritically expounded whenever questions about deteriorating standards of literacy are raised. The argument goes that if standards are declining, it must be because teachers are not teaching grammar: it assumes that there is a direct causal relation between competence in writing and knowledge of grammar.

The analogous counter-argument which is frequently marshalled is that we do not need to know precisely how a car works in order to drive it. Nor do we need to understand the physiology of the human balance mechanism, or the workings of gears, in order to ride a bicycle. However, for many people, it is only in driving a car that they become interested at all in how one works, and then only so far, just enough to satisfy a particular need. This may be especially true when something goes wrong. Drivers do not need specialist engineering knowledge, but there are some things they may need to know in certain circumstances, or are interested in knowing purely for interest's sake.

To take this analogy into language, being able to use language with pleasure and some success may bring about an interest in how language works, but knowledge of how it works is certainly not a prerequisite for fluency and is not the main element in teaching effective writing. One of the problems is that there is little research evidence to draw on because the relation of children's knowledge about grammar to their proficiency in language has received relatively little attention. What evidence there is seems to be flawed, and as David Tomlinson (1994) argues, many of the studies turn out to be little more than polemic:

> They (researchers and supervisors) are usually so convinced in their own minds that grammar teaching is pointless that, as long as the research findings are consonant with their opinions, they do not look closely at how those findings are obtained. (p. 20)

Tomlinson was asked to submit a paper to the National Curriculum Council. His summary of that paper is to be found in *English in Education* (Tomlinson 1994). This paper reports his investigation of two influential and much cited research projects on the teaching of formal grammar, one an MEd dissertation and the other a PhD thesis, neither of which was formally published and both of which, he argues, are methodologically flawed. The main question he raises relates to the meaning of 'formal grammar teaching', which both researchers claimed to be investigating: Does it mean the formal teaching of grammar, or the teaching of formal grammar?

In the more significant piece of research of the two (Harris 1962), secondary school children across five London schools were given formal grammar lessons, using a traditional textbook; their written compositions were assessed and then compared with a control group ostensibly taught no grammar, but which did have a writing class each week. However, Tomlinson points out that this control group was invalid because the children were in fact taught about grammar, although not in the formal way of the main group. Although they did not have separate lessons on grammar, their teacher discussed their work with them and drew attention to grammatical features, such as the re-phrasing of a sentence, without recourse to the formal terminology of grammar. In addition, in some of the schools it was necessary for the same teacher to take both groups; Tomlinson argues that it is inconceivable that these teachers adopted entirely different approaches to each class. He concludes that it is misleading to label the control groups as non-grammar groups and that the findings – that the non-grammar classes tended to improve because they were given more practice in writing – are therefore invalid in respect of the research carried out.

Similarly, research by Macauley, carried out over 50 years ago, is often referred to as evidence of the uselessness of formal grammar teaching. In his article 'The difficulty of grammar' (1947) he set out to assess to what extent children knew the parts of speech. His tests showed that on the whole children did not know them, except, not surprisingly, for children in the top sets. However, the only conclusion that can be drawn from his work is that teaching a particular kind of grammar was a waste of time – the study focused on children's knowledge of word classes (being able to identify parts of speech), rather than on syntax. In later studies, where children were asked to identify larger units of language which would constitute the core pattern of a sentence, the results were much better. That is to say, looking at isolated words and being able to say what part of speech they are is not a good indicator of grammatical knowledge. Looking at the meaning of a whole unit of language, such as a sentence, and identifying what the main grammatical processes are, is more relevant.

Hudson (2000) summarises the debates about whether there is any benefit to writing competence from teaching grammar and concludes that the question is still open, since he discusses studies which suggest there is and there isn't. There is clearly a need for more research into this issue, and particularly in relation to beginning writers and readers, because most of the research that does exist, however dated, refers to secondary age pupils and public examination success.

Both the examples above show that research into the teaching of grammar and its effects on the learner is interesting but often flawed by poor methodologies; results are sometimes used to endorse teaching practices which do not stand up to scrutiny. It may be useful at this point to remind ourselves what 'grammar' actually is. Grammar is the system of rules by which parts of words, words and sentences combine and relate to make meaning. It encompasses **syntax** (the structural relations of words and parts of words), **phonology** (the study of the sounds of a language), and **semantics** (the study of the meanings of words and sentences).

A second significant aspect of the public debate about grammar is revealed here: 'grammar' means different things to different people. The definition I offer above is the linguist's technical definition. It differs from what we might call the popular or commonsense view which holds that grammar is *correct* English, and correct grammar is the grammar of standard written English. This view is associated with an approach to teaching which is prescriptive, non-relative and based on written forms. This has come to be called the traditional approach: the teaching of decontextualised Latinate grammar which focuses on small units of language, usually at the level of the sentence, clause and phrase. These two views clearly come into conflict and are at the root of many misunderstandings and arguments about how language should be taught. There is a huge gap between linguists and ordinary people and this gulf is about more than which textbooks should be used. It relates to the associations and symbolism surrounding the very word 'grammar' and has led to what has been called a *moral panic*. Cameron (1995), in her analysis of the nature of this moral panic inherent in the debate about the teaching of grammar, argues that grammar is

> the metaphorical correlate for a cluster of related political and moral terms: order, tradition, authority, hierarchy and rules . . . A panic about grammar is therefore interpretable as the metaphorical expression of persistent conservative fears that we are losing the values that underpin civilisation and sliding into chaos. (p. 95)

A further significant feature of the debate about the teaching of grammar is that grammar and Standard English are treated as co-terminous, that is that grammar and Standard English mean the same thing. This implies that other dialects do not have grammars. Standard English is an important dialect with high status and prestige, and in its spoken form it is the closest English dialect to formal written English. But it is nevertheless a dialect, which some non-linguists find rather surprising because the word dialect has come to be associated only with non-standard forms. Many English speakers believe that they do not have a dialect.

The connotations of the word 'standard' also have a bearing on popular attitudes to Standard English. It has developed status through its associations with words such as 'standards' and expressions such as 'up to standard'. We all know how important standards are, especially now that there are standards in education for most things. But standard has a less prestigious orientation too, such as when it is used in 'standard train ticket' and 'standard shoe size'. Nevertheless, the associations remain.

It is striking how many people, particularly journalists and politicians, feel they have an expert understanding of English and the best way to teach it, and that they are entitled to express opinions on it. English attracts these 'experts' more than any other subject in the curriculum, perhaps because its specialist nature is not as apparent as that of science or mathematics. We speak and write English and therefore feel qualified to comment on how it should be taught. People are keen to make judgements about language use, especially in terms of the perceived deterioration in standards since some unspecified golden age of education. These tendencies do not seem to be as strong in other curriculum areas, like mathematics, though of course the debate about mental arithmetic, computers and children's ability to recite the multiplication tables rages on. The difference is that in mathematics it is not such a moral crusade. Not only is it seen as necessary to ensure that grammar is attended to so that children can learn to write, but correctness in the use of language, by which is meant the ability to produce the forms of Standard English, is equated with the moral standards of the nation. When people are careless or inaccurate about spelling and punctuation, or make 'mistakes' in grammatical forms, the nation is seen to be at risk. If citizens do not conform to the accepted norms of linguistic behaviour, they are in effect rejecting the laws of their society and challenging authority, not showing respect for the values of that society. It seems that 'we was' is capable of bringing down an empire. Now that the more traditional approach to the teaching of the grammar of English (parsing, clause analysis, exercises and drills) is no longer common, teachers are blamed for the demise in moral responsibility of British citizens, as this quotation demonstrates:

> Attitudes to the rules of grammar and care in the choice of words encourages punctiliousness in other matters. The overthrow of grammar coincided with the acceptance of the equivalent of creative writing in social behaviour. As nice points of grammar were mockingly dismissed as pedantic and irrelevant, so was punctiliousness in matters of honesty, responsibility, property, gratitude, apology, and so on. (John Rae, *Observer*, 7 February 1982)

Rae is arguing that allowing children more freedom in how and what they write, and not insisting on certain points of grammar, leads to a lowering of standards of moral behaviour. Actually, he is stating this, rather than arguing it, which is typical of the style of the whole debate, where positions are adopted, never properly argued and certainly never relinquished.

The above comments represent what I would call a commonsense view of language teaching, which conflicts with many teachers' views about how and why language and literacy should be taught. The commonsense view has two complementary thrusts: firstly, that teachers must identify poor, sloppy and incorrect usage not necessarily to improve standards but to prevent a decline in the moral fibre of the nation; and secondly, that we must prevent deterioration through change and succeed in fixing the language. If we stop language from changing we can polish up what we have until it shines.

In relation to the first of these points, I do not know any teachers who believe they should do nothing whatsoever about identifying poor, sloppy and incorrect English. However, this does raise a number of questions: what counts as poor, as sloppy, as incorrect? Who decides? What kind of grammar should be taught and for what purpose? Which methods are best suited to developing children's understanding about language? The call for a return to exercises and drills implied in many public comments is resisted strongly by the teaching profession, by linguists, and in reports such as the *Report of the Committee of Enquiry into the*

Teaching of English Language (Kingman Report, DES 1988), which stated that it did not recommend a return to grammar teaching based on a model of language derived from Latin rather than English. The report also argued that the two extreme viewpoints about the teaching of grammar – at one end, 'drill them in grammar' and at the other 'teach them nothing about grammar' – were misguided.

The second point, about preventing deterioration, is closely linked with the first, the correction of errors and sloppiness. Together, they form the basis of the complaint tradition. As the English language became established and standardised, there has been a related history of linguistic complaint in England, charted in some detail by Crowley (1991) and Milroy and Milroy (1985). Medieval concerns about language focused largely on the growth of English to replace French and on the relative status of each. As English was elaborated to meet new functions in public life, there followed a process of codification and standardisation; such rapid changes and developments germinated the seeds of the complaint tradition which flourishes today. One influential example of this is William Caxton's complaint about the extent of linguistic diversity in English and the problems this caused him as a printer:

> And certaynly our language now vsed varyeth ferre from that whiche was vsed and spoken whan I was borne . . . And that comyn Englysshe that is spoken in one shyre varyeth from a nother . . . a mercer cam in-to an hows and axed for mete [food]; and specyally he axyd after eggyes: And the goode wyf answerde, that she coude not speke no Frenshe. And the marchaunt was angry, for he also coude speke no Frenshe, but wolde haue egges, and she vnderstode hym not. And thenne at laste a nother sayd that he wolde haue eyren: then the good wyf sayd that she vnderstod hym wel. Loo, what sholde a man in thyse dayes now wryte, egges or eyren. Certaynly, it is harde to playse eueryman by cause of dyuersite and chaunge of language. (quoted in Harris and Taylor 1980, p. 86)

People from different parts of the country would have had considerable difficulty in understanding each other, not just in terms of accents, which may cause problems even today, but particualrly in terms of dialect, that is, grammar and vocabulary. Caxton's comments indicate his frustration as a printer in deciding which form of English to use and the problems caused when multiple forms exist in one small geographical region. In selecting the form used in the south-east of England, he chose a version of English which was already politically and commercially strong and which was to become the basis of modern Standard English. It is interesting to speculate what English would be like today if he had selected the dialect of the north-west.

From Caxton to the present day, there is a tradition of complaint about English. From the fourteenth to the sixteenth centuries such comments were characterised by a concern for the status of English in comparison with French, Latin or Greek, and it was only when English became confirmed as the official language of the nation that comments began to be made about nuances of meaning, or the preferred order of words, or the exact use of a conjunction. Swift's *A Proposal for Correcting, Improving and Ascertaining the English Language*, published in 1712, is considered to be a classic of the tradition, with its call for a fixed standard language and an academy to police it. With unashamed sycophancy, he wrote to the Prime Minister:

> I must be so plain as to tell your Lordship, that if you will not take some care to settle our language, and put it into a state of continuance, I cannot promise that your memory shall be preserved above an hundred years, further than by imperfect tradition. (1957 edition, p. 17)

The complaint tradition thrives in the twentieth and twenty-first centuries. Milroy and Milroy (1985) divide complaints into two related categories: legalistic – concerned with correctness and often appealing to erroneous notions of logic, such as two negatives make a positive; and moralistic – concerned with the use of language to confuse and obfuscate. A contemporary example of the latter would be the many complaints made about the use of euphemisms in war reporting, most recently demonstrated in reporting the civil war in the Balkans: 'theatre of war', 'explosive device', 'ethnic cleansing'. In relation to education, however, it is the first of these categories, the legalistic, which is most evident. Implicit in both is a desire to protect language from detrimental change, or in fact, any change. Newspapers are good sources of examples of the complaint tradition. MacKinnon (1996) cites a number of complaints during 1993 and 1994 from the letters section of *The Times* about the state of the language. This one is fairly typical:

> Could we stop assuming that any noun can automatically be turned into a verb? To access may be a battle already lost, but I draw the line at to impact, heard last week. As for to 'outsource', words fail me. (1 January 1994)

Words clearly did not fail this writer, nor are words likely to as long as language grows to meet our needs. Such debates are a frequent feature of the letters pages in certain newspapers, where writers rail against what they see as the inadequacies, deficiencies and unacceptability of other people's English.

Another frequent objection is to the use of 'hopefully' in expressions such as 'hopefully, I will see you tomorrow'. The basis of the objection is that since hopefully is an adverb it must modify a verb, but in these cases does not: 'I won't see you in a hopeful way'. However, there are many examples of these **disjuncts**, adverbs that sit outside the clause, and they do not incur the same strength of feeling: *thankfully, it didn't rain: sadly, he passed away.* This demonstrates how people often turn to spurious grammatical 'rules' as a justification for personal preferences and prejudices. MacKinnon comments that he has little sympathy with

> those who insist on correctness in grammar, spelling and meaning without recognising that correctness depends totally on how language is used, that usages vary and change, and above all that even genuine mistakes are usually of little or no consequence. (p. 364)

When people make comments about others' uses of language, they are usually criticizing more than their language.

To return to my classroom where, as a new, inexperienced teacher, and in a political climate which seemed to require it, I was teaching a narrow form of knowledge about language, largely uncritically and certainly without any attention to the actual needs and interests of the children. I was treating language as a system divorced from use, and, as Mittens (1985) puts it, ironically echoing the poem by Henry Reed, I was doing 'the naming of parts'. The poem of this title, about soldiers' divided experiences of brutality and beauty, describes how a focus on the parts, in this case of a gun, neglects the whole, the horror of war and the way the world and seasons continue around the barbarity. In the same way, focusing on the parts of language could be said to have a similar effect – we forget the whole. I do not want to suggest that teaching about the English language has nothing whatever to do with the parts of speech, and nothing to do with understanding the conventions of Standard English. What I am suggesting, however, is that a narrow focus on forms gives children a narrow experience of what it means to study language. It makes them behave passively toward language rather than encouraging them to actively question, play with and investigate language. It presents language almost as synonymous with writing, whereas writing is only one use of language; it suggests that children have to be able to reproduce perfect written forms immediately, rather than recognising that, as children develop as language users, they go through transitional stages as they gradually shape language to their own enlarged and extended purposes.

A NEW AGENDA FOR TEACHING LANGUAGE?

The lack of an adequate agreement about what children should be taught about language has led successive governments to take action to settle the debate, most significantly in the establishment of a national curriculum for English at the end of the 1980s, and culminating in the implementation of the NLS. There is no doubt that guidance on the nature of the language curriculum was much needed, and that there were, and remain, strong public and political concerns about standards of literacy in the population generally. At a positive level, this has resulted in greater attention to language than existed before and in ensuring an entitlement of sorts for children. No matter which state school they attend there is more or less guaranteed coverage of the same syllabus and methodology. It is more or less because schools may make approved adaptations, but the point remains. In a less positive sense, it has resulted in a narrowing of options for teachers in relation to what and how to teach, as content and methodology become increasingly prescribed.

The implementation of the NLS has certainly raised the profile of literacy: or, rather, it has raised the profile of a particular view of literacy and how it is developed. The philosophy underpinning the NLS reflects a basic skills agenda.

In the Foreword to the Framework, the Secretary of State for Education and Employment states 'if children do not master the basic skills of literacy and numeracy while they are at primary school, they will be seriously disadvantaged later'. Literacy is clearly identified as a basic competence, a prerequisite for future success in education and life. This is presented as unproblematic and non-controversial: to be literate means to be able to read and write for basic purposes, a further example of the disjuncture between professional and 'commonsense' views.

A more developed and rounded view of literacy sees it as a set of practices which people use in their lives for many varied purposes, as distinct from being one acquired skill divorced from use. Literacy must deal with situations, contexts: it is applied knowledge and understanding in action. You have to have something to be literate with or about and literacy has to have outcomes beyond simply being able to read and write. The difficulty with this belief is that it is complex: it is personal, in that it relates to affective aspects of our lives, political in that it refers to the place and power of literacy in people's lives and challenging, because it questions how schools teach and develop it. If 'schooled' literacy prevails, a term which describes the narrow form of literacy taught in schools, then much is left out. Schooled literacy could be described as providing a limiting technology for children, rather than a life-enhancing and rewarding orientation to language. As Street (1994) has argued, 'The notion that the acquisition of a single, autonomous literacy will have pre-defined consequences for individuals and societies has been shown to be a myth, often premised on narrow culturally specific values about what is proper literacy'. Nevertheless, pedagogic debates do tend to circle around such narrow interpretations because the idea of an essential basic skill is so strongly embedded in our educational history.

THE CONTEXT OF SITUATION

Language is not a system in a vacuum. It exists because people use it, and it is the context of use which determines the kind of language we employ. The HMI publication *English 5–16*, written in 1984 as an initial proposal for a national curriculum for English, suggested a curriculum which included knowledge about language and an emphasis on the importance of audience and purpose in speech and writing. It recognised that forms of spoken and written language are determined by the context of their use and was one of the first strategy documents to emphasise a more relative view of correctness.

The report stressed that language is relative and this relativism was represented by the term 'appropriateness', a concept already embedded in educational discourse and which recognised that language users have to take into account what is appropriate to the context. This sounds simple enough but it leaves a good deal open to question, such as how we know what is appropriate and who decides. This term was used because it avoided the problematic notions of 'correctness', 'proper', and 'right and wrong'. It recognised that fluent language users know an immense amount about how to use language, how to adapt it to the context. By addressing language in use, it also dragged the study of English out of the textbook and placed it in the real world of literacy and oracy, of writing and reading, of talking and listening.

Many of these processes of choice and selection are invisible, so much part of our social and cultural knowledge that we do not realise we know them or have exercised any choice. We are acculturated into the discourse practices of our society and learn to use language according to its expectations and demands. Much of what we learn is absorbed as we grow up in a society, through interaction with other members, and we do not have to stop and think how to write or say it. Some of what we learn is expressly taught to us through the monitoring of our language: 'Don't speak like that to your grandmother'. Sometimes when we learn we are more conscious of the process, because we have to stop and think a little: how to word a letter to effect an apology yet not to lose face over the apology; how to adjust our 'normal' speech when talking to a young child. For all successful language users, the language has to be appropriate to the context, and it is important to recognise that this word 'context' does not simply refer to the physical situation: it encompasses a whole range of linguistic and extra-linguistic features, such as the relationships between the people involved, their purposes and the physical and non-verbal situations. The word itself has two roots: *con*, meaning with and *text*, the language used: context is all that accompanies, surrounds and precedes the language event.

Linguists use the term **context of situation** to describe the whole environment of a language event. The phrase was coined in 1923 by Bronislaw Malinowski, an anthropologist who carried out research in the Trobriand Islands in the South Pacific. His principal interest was in mapping the culture of the islanders, their practices, rituals, daily lives. In order to do this, he had to interpret and translate their language, Kiriwinian, and in doing so he found that literal translations could not convey the meaning of the original: he needed to understand both what was going on and the cultural context in which the speakers were operating. This was true both for very pragmatic contexts, such as fishing or harvesting, and for the interpretation of language which was more interpersonal, such as expressions of gratitude or hostility. The language could not be translated word for word because the translator needed to include the whole cultural history of the people – the way they framed and made sense of their world – in order to convey what the speakers actually meant. For example, the ways in which time or spacial relationships are marked differ between cultures, and a direct, literal translation from the language would not make any sense to an outsider. Malinowski made extensive notes about the context to accompany his linguistic work, placing the text in its actual environment so that a non-Kiriwinian speaker could obtain a truer understanding of what was taking place. This marked a significant development in the practice of anthropology.

Most speakers and writers take for granted that the context determines the language used. Imagine two people who have never met before sitting next to each other on a plane. How do they know what to say to each other? What is the context here? It is certainly not just a pressurised cabin. The context changes and shifts during the flight, as experiences and knowledge are shared. Sapir (1921), an American linguist and anthropologist working in the late nineteenth and early twentieth centuries, argued that language cannot exist apart from culture. By culture he meant the sets of practices, beliefs and systems which are the fabric of daily life.

Consciously and unconsciously we make choices from our available linguistic repertoires to create spoken and written texts, operating within conventions, and sometimes outside conventions so that new uses of language emerge. We take into account a whole range of features which comprise the context and we construct our written or spoken discourses accordingly.

A STRUCTURALIST MODEL OF LANGUAGE

The way I was teaching language in my early teaching days might be described as conforming to a structuralist model: it treated language as an autonomous mechanism with cogs and pulleys called **sentences**, **phonemes** and **morphemes**. It had its origins in the post-Renaissance period, when, perhaps surprisingly, the main players in the study of language were scientists, trying to render language amenable to rational analysis in the way that the study of the natural world was also being treated. One highly influential book, *The Rudiments of English Grammar* (1761) was written by Joseph Priestley, the chemist who discovered oxygen. This may not be as strange as it seems. It is not too difficult to see a similarity between grammar and chemistry: both are transformational, combining units to make new units, with words and their parts, and molecules and their parts, the building bricks in each discipline. Just as molecules combine to form compounds, so morphemes (the parts that words are made from) combine to form words.

The purpose of such early grammar books was to standardise, to identify and to describe the English language so as to set the standard for future generations and across the world. Samuel Johnson's dictionary, begun in 1747 and published in 1755, was intended to contribute to this process of standardisation, to fix meaning and spelling and to preserve the 'purity' of the language. This Johnson expounded in his *Plan of a Dictionary of the English Language* in 1747:

> The chief intent of it is to preserve the purity and ascertain the meaning of our English idiom . . . tongues, like governments, have a natural tendency to degeneration: we have long preserved our constitution, let us make some struggles for our language. (Preface)

By the time the dictionary was finished, Johnson was rather less sanguine about the possibility of achieving this, and he came to see that fixing and preserving a language was an illusion:

We laugh at the elixir that promises to prolong life to a thousand years: and with equal justice may the lexicographer be derided, who being able to produce no example of a nation that has preserved their words and phrases from mutability, shall imagine that his dictionary can embalm his language and secure it from corruption and decay. (cited in Jackson 1988, p. 116)

The actual methodology by which his dictionary entries were collected and constructed was highly idiosyncratic, if not illegitimate: it contains examples of Johnson inventing definitions and displaying personal invective against things or people he despised, as the following entries demonstrate:

> *patron:* commonly a wretch who supports with insolence, and is paid with flattery.
> *oats:* a grain which in England is commonly given to horses but in Scotland supports the people.
> *lexicographer:* a harmless drudge.
> *irony:* a mode of speech in which the meaning is contrary to the words, as in *Bolingbroke was a holy man.*

Entries like these, and the fact that Johnson used literature, not examples of actual speech, as his sources, do provide a little ammunition against pedants who cite dictionaries as the definitive authorities on meaning and usage. Problems with dictionary entries are not confined to older dictionaries. In 1996, the Microsoft Spanish dictionary for Word versions 6 and 7 was severely criticised for its racist and sexist definitions. Synonyms for 'indigenous person' were 'cannibal' and 'savage'; for 'westerner' 'civilised' and 'cultured'. Microsoft had used an out-of-date dictionary to create this database.

Linguists in the nineteenth century, influenced by developments in scientific knowledge, particularly in the area of evolution (Darwin's *On the Origin of Species* was published in 1859), began to see language less from a mathematical perspective and more as an organic entity, that is, to view language as living and subject to natural laws. They began to be interested in the way languages of the world interrelate, in the history and evolution of the world's languages, and to see language as living, dynamic and evolving over time. This marked a gradual shift in theoretical perspective.

SAUSSURE AND CHOMSKY

The two most significant linguists this century in terms of their contribution to structuralist theory are Ferdinand de Saussure (1857–1913) and Noam Chomsky (1928–). Their influence lies in the distinctions they made between **langue** and **parole** (Saussure) and **competence** and **performance** (Chomsky)

'Langue' was Saussure's term for the conventions or rules of a language which speakers have the potential to utilise but which they may not consciously know or even actually use. This idealised form of the language is realised through what he called 'parole', individual utterances made by speakers. We deduce langue from the way it manifests itself in actual speech. Langue determines parole, yet has no concrete existence of its own. Because parole requires actual speakers, the study of language from a purely historical perspective will not be adequate. Saussure insisted that the study of language must be undertaken not only diachronically, but also from a synchronic perspective, which means the study of language at a particular point in time. This ensured that a language's historical dimension was no longer prioritised over its structural features. Saussure's influence spread from the posthumous publication in 1916 of his lectures at the University of Geneva, compiled from students' notes under the title *Course in General Linguistics*.

Langue and parole have counterparts in Chomsky's concepts of competence and performance. Writing in the American linguistic tradition (his influential work *Syntactic Structures* was published in 1957) Chomsky argued that the true object of study for the linguist was not the imperfect, halting, incomplete language uttered by speakers (performance), but the underlying knowledge which any speaker of a language possesses (competence).

> Linguistic theory is concerned primarily with an ideal speaker-listener, in a completely homogeneous speech community, who knows its language perfectly and is unaffected by such grammatically irrelevant conditions as memory limitations, distractions, shifts of attention and interest, and errors in applying his [sic] knowledge of the language in actual performance. (Chomsky 1965, p. 3)

Speakers have implicit knowledge of a set of rules for transforming units of language into innumerable other forms, a process Chomsky called **transformational generative grammar**. This grammar provides all the processes needed to produce all potential sentences in a language. Chomsky distinguished the deep structure of a language, which he claimed all languages share, from the surface structure, the description of how languages diverge in actual use.

The ability to compute, or transform, the language is a speaker's competence, which is realised through performance, and it is this competence which is of interest to the linguist – a return of sorts to the mathematical orientations of an earlier age. Chomsky argued that the brain is pre-programmed to carry out these linguistic operations, through what he termed its 'language acquisition device' (LAD).

A FUNCTIONAL MODEL OF LANGUAGE

The significance of the work of Saussure and Chomsky in relation to my early teaching lies in their emphasis on language as an autonomous system. This provided an inadequate theory for teaching about language because it takes no account of language as embedded in and determined by the context of situation:

it took the people out of language. It neglected any consideration of the functions of language and of how and why language varies in speech and writing. This leads us into a consideration of the alternative to the language model I was using – towards a theory which recognises that language is not fixed and unchanging, but is dynamic, and fulfils all the functions necessary for its speakers. This functional model of language has come to be associated with the work of M. A. K. Halliday. It has become very influential in education in the UK, but also particularly in Australia, where he has done most of his work.

A functional theory of language recognises the context of situation. It is based on the theory that the structure of language – of words, sentences, paragraphs and so on – is derived from its function. There is always a purpose which both drives and reflects the form language takes. The context not only determines what we say; what we say becomes itself part of the context. Halliday introduced the terms **field**, **tenor** and **mode** to describe the central facets of the context of situation. Field is what is happening, what the activity entails and the purpose which it is serving. Tenor is the relationship between the persons who are participating, whether they are readers and writers or speakers and listeners. Mode is the means through and by which the language situation or event is conducted – a letter, a book, an article, a phone call, a Web site, and so on. Halliday gives as an example Nigel, aged 11 months, in the bathroom with his mother. The field is bathing and washing and playing with containers and wanting other people's things (a toothbrush belonging to his father). The tenor is a mother/child interaction, where the adult is using opportunities to teach the child ('I think the frog is too big for the mug'). The mode is a conversation accompanying action.

In this theory, the language used by participants in a language event is described in terms of its function. This is the determining feature of Halliday's philosophy of language. He argues that a functional model of language needs to account for variation in language. Language varies in three significant dimensions: **dialectically, diatypically and diachronically**. A model of language for an educational context demands a theory of language which recognises and explores these dimensions. This model would recognise that variation is the norm; that we all use a variety of dialects (regional and social) and a variety of **registers**; and that none of these is ever fixed or unchanging, as the complaint tradition assumes.

Halliday's (1978) proposal for a functional model means that we need to look at the functions of language, its purposes and effects, the relation of form to function and at what language can actually do, rather than focusing exclusively on its forms and structures. Before we go further, however, the terms **dialectal**, **diatypic** and **diachronic** require some explanation.

Dialectal variety means that language varies because of the language user. Speakers or writers may use a particular form of language, including international versions of English such as American English or Australian English. They may use a regional or class dialect (sometimes called a **sociolect**) or accent. Here dialect refers to grammatical, lexical and syntactical variants whereas accent refers only to pronunciation, although the two are not always so easily distinguishable: for example 'innit' could be seen as a dialect feature of London English and also as a feature of that accent, as a pronunciation of 'isn't it'. Dialectal variety accounts for regional and social variations in language use, and encompasses issues such as gender, ethnicity and class. Dialectal variety also refers to written language, in that writers may write in a particular way because of who they are, though the main relevance here is to spoken language. The emphasis is on the user of language.

Diatypic variety refers to the way language varies according to the uses to which it is put. A report written by the chair of a governing body to parents is very different from a newspaper report of a football match; a bill from British Telecom is different from the one a window cleaner leaves; an acceptance speech for a Nobel prize is very different from one for an Oscar. These are all examples of diatypic variety, forms of language which are determined by purposes and context. They differ because of linguistic and social convention ('the way we do things here'), because of levels of formality, relationships between the participants, because of what is being done at the time. Halliday (Halliday and Hasan 1985) describes the difference between a dialect and a diatype, or register, in this way:

> In principal, dialects are saying the same thing in different ways, whereas registers are saying different things . . . whereas in principle at least, any individual might go through life speaking only one dialect (in modern complex societies this is increasingly unlikely; but it is theoretically possible and it used to be the norm), it is not possible to go through life using only one register. (p. 41)

The third aspect of variation is diachronic variation, the way language changes over time. This can occur at a number of levels. At the level of lexis, changes occur for three principle reasons: borrowings, innovations (**neologisms** arising from a need for new words particularly in areas such as technology), invasions and immigration. Here are some examples of lexical change:

- Changes of actual meaning over a short or long period. For example, the word *silly*, or *saelig* in Old English, meant happy or blessed; in the Middle English period its meaning had shifted to innocent; and now in Modern English it has a range of meanings including foolish, stupid and ignorant. Within a much shorter timescale we can see that the meanings of words like *acid*, *gay* and *rave*, have significantly changed.
- Words taken from other languages now part of the word stock of English (**loan words**), such as *anorak* (Inuit), *manifesto* (Italian), *mumps* (Icelandic).
- Words which had longer forms which are now rarely used, with the **clipped form** now predominant, such as *lab, zoo, phone*.
- Words which have narrowed their meaning, such as *accident*, which originally meant any actual event, but now means something unintended and usually

undesired, and *meat* which originally meant any food, but now is specific to animal flesh.

- Words which have widened their meaning, such as *manufactured*, which originally meant made by hand.
- Words which have completely reversed their meaning, though these are not very many. For example, the Anglo-Saxon word *wan* meant dark, whereas now it means pale or colourless.
- Words that are abbreviations but which have become acronyms, that is they are pronounced as words: AIDS, NATO, UNICEF.
- Fad words, which rise and fall quickly according to social changes, such as words associated with boom and bust economies in the 1980s, like *dinkies* (double income, no kids). I suspect that the word *yuppy* may still survive as a perjorative term but it has not embedded itself in the lexis, and *nilks* (no income, lots of kids), though highly relevant to contemporary life, has never caught on.

Diachronic change occurs in areas other than lexis: for example:

- In grammar, such as verb forms – Pepys writes *my wife come to see me at Whitehall.*
- In conventions of pronunciation – some accents, such as **received pronunciation** (RP) have significantly changed, as we can hear in radio programmes from the 1950s.
- In graphology – for example the use of capitalisation in the seventeenth century, and the loss of the Old English and Icelandic runic letter *thorn*, which is where we get the word *ye* from in *ye olde tea shoppe*, a misreading of this letter, because it looked like *y* – but was pronounced as *th*.
- In discourse, where the appropriateness of a particular kind of writing changes (note, for example, the linguistic implications in writing e-mail texts).

INTERPERSONAL AND IDEATIONAL ASPECTS OF THE FUNCTIONAL MODEL

Halliday (1978) also draws an important distinction between the **ideational** and the **interpersonal** functions of language. When speakers use language, they represent and express, there is content. This is the ideational function of language. But just as importantly, there is an interpersonal aspect, which is to do with the relationships between participants in the situation. Through language, relationships are established, maintained, changed and destroyed. For adult speakers, both functions operate at the same time: this means that any utterance conveys both content and a relationship to the content and to the addressee. We might call this colloquially 'attitude', though it is deeper than perhaps this word suggests.

Examples of the nature of this relationship are relative status (who is important and powerful and who isn't), or how receptive participants are to each other (friendly or hostile). Halliday argues that very young children operate with either ideational or interpersonal functions in any speech event, but not both. Gradually, at around 24 months, they come to be combined, as in adult speech.

A FUNCTIONAL MODEL IN PRACTICE

For teaching purposes, any model of language must take into account:

- that language is functional;
- that language varies and the nature of that variation;
- that language does far more than transmit information.

A variational, functional model of language is entirely relevant in the primary school. It opens up a whole world of language use which children need to come to understand, and this awareness must be fostered in the primary years, particularly the later years. The ability to use and understand a wide range of language varieties must be a major goal of the language curriculum, in order that children develop competence in the linguistic demands that are and will be made on them. A developing competence in language and critical reflection on language are complementary, interrelated aspects of children's growth in, and through, language. Where, then, do we begin in applying the model to learning about language in the classroom?

First, there is an essential distinction to be drawn between what children know **implicitly** about language, and what they can come to know **explicitly**. Consider these two pieces of writing by Laura, the first at age four years and three months, the second a year later.

> to Rubeca
> IcAptBiying sic
> Buttha was soonowv with
> thank you for the cad
> rBaca
> love from Laura
> (translation)
> to Rebecca
> I kept being sick but that was soon over with. Thank you for the card Rebecca. Love from Laura.

This first piece of writing shows Laura's early understanding of how to use written forms to make meaning. She uses:

- phonic knowledge to approximate to the sounds of words: *rubeca/rbaca;*
- graphic or visual knowledge learned from reading, to approximate to the shape, pattern and length of words: *biying;*
- graphic knowledge of upper and lower case letters and beginning understanding about the separation of words;

- textual knowledge of the layout of a letter: *to/love from;*
- textual knowledge of the functions of a particular text, the kind of thing one writes in a thank you letter.

Laura is learning how to mean, a term Gordon Wells uses for children's early learning of language to make meanings. Wells (1986) charts the early language lives of children in the Bristol Study, 'Language at Home and at School', a long-term research project which followed children from infancy to the end of their primary education and focused on how they used and learned language for communicating and for making sense of their worlds. This sample of Laura's language shows her developing understanding of language at a number of levels: morphological (words and their structure), syntactical (words and their relationships) and textual (making a text from words and sentences). She is learning the discourses that her culture uses, one of many literacy practices that she needs to accomplish.

Laura's text reveals her developing implicit understanding of language. It is implicit because it is unconscious learning, brought about by her engagement with the world of home and nursery, where she sees language in operation, used by people for real purposes, and then makes sense of it by producing some of her own. Laura has not learned to do this entirely by chance, by absorbing it from her environment. There are probably elements which will have been demonstrated and explained to her, particularly if she has received letters herself. There may even be aspects of what she has written which she explicitly understands and can explain, such as the conventions of letter writing (she was able to explain the signing off conventions such as 'love from', for example). Largely, however, her knowledge of how language works remains implicit and this text can be seen as evidence of her growing language competence, where implicit knowledge is used and practised.

Implicit knowledge enables us to distinguish grammatical sequences of words from ungrammatical ones. We know that 'Yesterday I will sort out the problem' and 'Bus the coming is', do not make sense, even though we may not have the linguistic terminology to explain what is wrong. We have never heard such formulations from other speakers of our language. We test these forms against what we already know and quickly realise that such permutations are not possible. All of this is achieved without our necessarily being able to articulate what makes these expressions ungrammatical. Implicit knowledge is our native competence, or, as Richmond (1990) puts it 'Pupils' language competence is their implicit knowledge put to work' (p. 28).

Laura's second text, written twelve months after the first, reveals a different kind of awareness of the workings of language, that is, explicit knowledge.

dear rebeca
What hows ways next to nothing?
answer a light hous
What did the pliceman say to his tummy?
Stop your under a vest

Laura is aware that words can have more than one meaning. She exploits this by writing a joke and shows that she has understood:

- the nature of homonyms (words which sound the same but have different meanings);
- the generic question and answer structure of many jokes.

It is unlikely that at five Laura fully understands **homonyms**, but she knows that the word 'light' can be used in two different grammatical ways. Nor is it likely that she has the terminology to explain what makes a joke a joke. Nevertheless, this example shows a child on the move in terms of her knowledge about language. She is moving from an implicit to a more explicit understanding of language, demonstrating through jokes an appreciation of aspects of the forms and functions of language. Laura gets the jokes, and, through playing with language in this way, is able to look at language in a more objective way, as a system. In fact, jokes often play a pivotal role in children's developing awareness of the potential of language, as they explore how they can play with semantic ambiguity. Meek (1988) relates children's ability to play around with words to their development as readers as they exploit the potential of words to mean more than one thing, or put together words which would not normally go together (semantic incongruity): 'When they have learnt the rules, children know how to subvert them. A joke is often the best reading test' (p. 19).

Four years later (aged nine), Laura developed a quite sophisticated and extensive explicit knowledge about language. She could independently engage in a wide range of writing activities, such as taking orders for breakfast on a notepad, writing extended diary entries, publishing a cartoon strip and sending postcards from her holiday.

The difference between implicit and explicit knowledge about language seems, at first consideration, to be fairly straightforward. These terms are often used as if they are entirely separate, all or nothing concepts, so that implicit knowledge about language means demonstrating knowledge through use, but not being able to understand in a **metacognitive** way what it is you are doing, whereas explicit knowledge means you know enough about it to explain it cogently to someone else. You know something either implicitly or explicitly. I find these definitions problematic for two reasons. First, implicit knowledge about language is characterised as a kind of mindless, behaviouristic activity where children simply pour forth all that they have absorbed from the culture about using language. I would argue that implicit knowledge about language can involve a level of thinking about choices and appropriateness, particularly in writing, which is of a higher cognitive order. For example, to write a word, they may draw on a memory of spelling rules, or patterns in other similar words they can visualise, and will bring these complex processes to bear on what they actually write. This is quite different from unthinking spilling out of implicit knowledge.

Secondly, how explicit does explicit knowledge about language need to be, in order to count? Do you have to be able to explain it fully, using appropriate terminology? To whom need it be explained? Does it become explicit the moment you begin to talk about it, or is there a kind of sliding scale of explicitness as understanding emerges? Perhaps it is more helpful to think of a continuum of implicit understanding about language, with points on the continuum where things become more explicit for the learner.

THE QUESTION OF TERMINOLOGY

If we want to build on children's implicit knowledge and understanding of language, we will need to consider the question of terminology. Which technical terms are useful or essential for learning language and how should they be introduced and used? There have been debates for decades about whether children need any terminology at all to develop their language. Some teachers and researchers have argued that as long as the concept is understood, what it is called is not really relevant. It is certainly the case that knowing the technical term for something does not necessarily mean that one understands the thing it refers to. I know words like fusion and fission, but have little idea what they actually mean. It is important to recognise that knowing the terminology does not in itself guarantee understanding, particularly where the term refers to a process, such as in linguistics, the process of **nominalisation**. However, I would argue that knowing that term can enhance one's understanding by framing the concept, providing a means for talking about it. Linguistic terms form part of children's developing vocabulary: some will have very precise contexts for use and some will transfer into their daily lives. I refer here to terms such as text, author, dialogue, whereas terms such as hyphen, or alliteration are unlikely to make this transfer very often! Linguistic terminology is, in essence, no different from the terminology necessary in all subjects and disciplines, yet it seems to create much greater controversy and anxiety.

The important pedagogic principle about the teaching of terminology is that a pattern of experience needs to be established before the term is introduced. Children need to encounter the concept, then the term. For example, the NLS requires children to use synonyms in Year 2 before using the term themselves in Year 3, term 1. I think this sounds rather strange, since teachers are unlikely to withold the term in Year 2, but it indicates that by Year 3 children should be able to use the terminology independently.

It may be that the notion of terminology has come to be negatively associated with traditional methods for teaching language, that is, exercises and drills. It may also be the case that arguments against using linguistic terminology have become muddled with arguments about the purposes of learning about language: that it is only about the teaching of discrete, decontextualised bits of language, and that in fact it is about teaching terminology at the expense of other important things.

A recent experience serves as an example of this. During a visit to a Year 2 literacy hour, I asked the children what they were doing. 'Phonemes' came the reply. They were skimming through a selection of books from a well-known reading scheme to find the graphemes that make the phoneme 'er', as pronounced in the word 'fur'. The book the children were looking at was quite well illustrated and funny, but the children had not read it, so they didn't know how good it was. I presume the lesson plan was to cover 'the common spelling patterns for the vowel phonemes *er.*' The discussion was very lively.

> I've found one...'Peter' [I wondered about this. Perhaps it is the neutral vowel?]
> Me too. 'Turn'.
> I've got 'chimney' [pronounced chim-er-ney by the child].

I had some doubts about this activity and whether the children had a sufficiently grounded knowledge to carry it out. Some of them were learning things that were wrong. I cite this example because it typifies the complexity of using terminology in teaching language. The children knew the word for what they were looking for, but had an insecure grasp of the concept. Some terms, particularly those for the parts of speech, have formulaic definitions which can cause confusion for children. For example, calling a verb a *doing word*, as is commonly the case, can be problematic when we consider verbs like *be, die* or *sleep.* In what sense are these doing? Similarly, passive constructions, as in 'He was struck by lightning' do not seem to involve doing on the part of the subject of the sentence. Verbs are words which refer to actions, states and events: this fuller definition may be useful for some children. Nouns, often defined as the names of things, can be more fully described by considering classes of nouns: common nouns (which sub-divide into concrete, abstract and collective nouns), and proper nouns. The terms to be used need to be agreed in a school language policy, to reduce confusion for the learner and to provide a consistent approach to children's understanding about language.

It is important to recognise two principles in the use of terminology:

- not all children will need the same terms at the same time;
- some terms, but not all, will arise from discussing children's own work. Teachers will need to create contexts in which linguistic concepts and terminology can be directly taught, primarily to introduce them in an already understood context.

The following terms, drawn from a broad range of language areas, provide a suggested list for the primary years. The categories are not hard and fast but rather loose groupings to give a shape to the list. By the time they move into secondary school, children should have experience of hearing and using these terms:

Spoken language

language	dialect	accent	multilingual
bilingual	Standard English	dialogue	

Literary and figurative uses

narrative	narrator	author	text
character	setting	plot	sub-plot
rhythm	rhyme	metaphor	simile
assonance	alliteration	idiom	verse
stress	imagery	cliché	slang

Punctuation

question mark	exclamation mark	full stop	capital (upper case) letter
comma	inverted commas	apostrophe	small (lower case) letter
semi-colon	colon	quotation marks	

Parts of speech

noun: common: collective, abstract, concrete
noun: proper
         count, non-count
verb: tense, past, present, future
pronoun, adjective, adverb, conjunction, preposition

In the sentence and beyond

sentence	phrase	subject	object
paragraph	definite article	indefinite article	vowel
consonant			

Words and their meanings

singular	plural	prefix	suffix
comparative	superlative	synonym	antonym
homonym	homograph	homophone	syllable

Books

contents	chapter	index	caption
heading	catalogue	dictionary	thesaurus

Reading process

infer	skim	scan	reader
novel	information book	fiction	non-fiction

Writing process

brainstorm	plan	draft	edit
proof-read	publish	audience	purpose

Principles of languag[e]

Te[a]

28

handling of a

the same d[e]

learning

devel[o]

sim

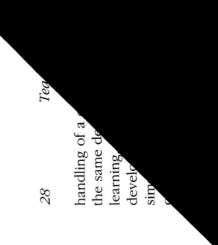

It is important to point out that a number of thes[e]
of language belong to particular linguistic scho[ol]
be accepted as definitive terms, but there are n[e]
linguistics which are not represented here, nor
example, much interesting work on noun phra[se]
to describe the lead word in a phrase which its[e]
In the following sentence: *Commuters from the s[outh]
as train companies fail to meet their targets,* the
of the noun phrase *commuters from the south*
valuable classroom activities on the noun phra[se]
inevitably lag behind developments in the disci[pline]
be transition points as teachers learn about ar[d]
things. There is a fascinating research project to be undertaken into the relation
between linguistics and its application in education.

In addition to the terminology above, the NLS, with its emphasis on a phonic
approach to the teaching of reading identifies a number of phonic reading skills
which children must learn, which introduces another set of terms to be
considered. It follows that children will begin to use them, as in the phoneme
example above, though it must be recognised that these belong to a very narrow
area of children's experience, that is, their early reading development, before
fluency is achieved. These are explained in the Glossary.

Essential phonic terminology

phoneme	blend	digraph	
grapheme	segment	onset	rime

It needs also to be emphasised that the terminology teachers need is more
extensive than the terminology children will need. Teachers need more, and
different knowledge in order to be confident in developing children's
understanding of language, though many teachers do feel quite uncertain in this
area, partly because of their own experiences at school. The knowledge they
need draws on a wide range of linguistic and sociolinguistic concepts; children's
knowledge is an appropriate selection from this range.

PEDAGOGIC PRINCIPLES FOR DEVELOPING CHILDREN'S KNOWLEDGE ABOUT LANGUAGE

In helping children to understand language better, it will be necessary to
scaffold their learning. This pedagogic concept has become influential in
educational practice and research (Bruner 1985; Wood *et al*. 1976). It refers to
the support given by an adult through which learners are assisted to achieve
something they would not have been able to achieve on their own. Scaffolding
enables learners to achieve a level of independent competence in a task, or

...oncept, so that they can be successful in it another time without ...gree of support. It refers to cognitive development, to goal-oriented ...with the adult acting to reduce the possibility of failure by staging the ...pment of the concept according to the learner's needs. It differs from ...ply helping learners in that help does not imply a didactic role on the part ...f the adult, whereas scaffolding does: the person who scaffolds intends to move learners through a process to the point where the support is no longer needed. Helping children to do a multiplication task is quite different in practice and effect from scaffolding their understanding of what they are doing, which might involve modelling processes, so that they grasp the mathematical concepts and can replicate them in another similar task. In helping, one either does the task for children or contributes to the completion of the task by taking it over. In scaffolding, however, the teacher does not take over complete control.

Scaffolding depends on the following elements:

- Teacher recognition of the stage of development that the child is going through and what the next stage of development might be. This demands both pedagogic and subject knowledge and a recognition of the child's actual and potential levels of achievement.
- Strategic and appropriate intervention and a recognition of the central importance of teachers' questions in the learning process. Questions should be used not simply to check that the child is on task ('How much more have you got to do?'), or to monitor or to ask the child to play back to you what has been done. They should be used to move the child on, to suggest avenues of enquiry, to create a changed context.
- The setting of tasks and activities which are differentiated and will challenge the learner, at whatever level they are working.
- A recognition that the intervention required can involve telling, showing, or demonstrating, and that these are important aspects of the teacher's scaffolding role.

Scaffolding is important in both incidental and focused attention to knowledge about language. When children collect examples of spoken language from around the school, the questions the teacher asks and the suggestions made about categorising the examples will enable the children to see the varying functions language has: a mass of information is shaped for and with the learner so that it begins to mean something. When the child reads out a story they have written, the discussion between teacher and child about ways of linking short sentences through subordination and coordination will scaffold the child's understanding. The teacher will decide whether and how to introduce linguistic terms like **conjunction** and **phrase** and will, for example, frame the concept for the child by saying 'we call this', or 'this is called'. Children's understanding will be confirmed through re-visiting the concept in another context. In this way a context is created in which reflection on language is fostered.

HOW SOON SHOULD CHILDREN BE TAUGHT ABOUT LANGUAGE?

Children's interest in language is evident from a very early age as they grapple with the language system and strive to make meaning through and of language. Learning about language does not begin when a teacher decides it should: children are learning about language implicitly and explicitly from a very early age. They ask what words mean and why people say the things they do and they learn how to cause trouble by saying the rude words they know in public. They learn that their name contains letters and that the marks they make on the page can have meaning. Parents and teachers support the child's inquisitiveness as competence develops, explaining meanings and monitoring and commenting on language used by the child.

Olsen (1984) argues that there are interesting and significant differences in the ways that parents talk about language to their children, that is, the extent to which they treat language as an object and use a language about language, a metalanguage. Parents who frame language for their children by talking about it with them are orientating their children to literacy. Olsen suggests that when children ask questions about language, such as 'What means "old-fashioned"?' or 'What means "by the way"?', they are showing a disposition toward language which treats it as an artefact, something to be examined, considered and learned about. If children are encouraged to treat language in this way, they are taking the first steps toward becoming literate. Activities in the home such as naming games (What's that? Bicycle!) using catalogues or a photograph album are as much about learning language (for example, that language names things), as they are about learning what things are. Olsen suggests that parents who play these games, and attend to language in a conscious way, are preparing their children for the conceptual and cognitive frames of schooled literacy.

The strange title of his article, '"See! Jumping!" some oral antecedents of literacy', comes from a mother's comments to her child while watching a frog jump in a pond. The mother uses these words to point out to the child what is happening in the pond, but she is trying at the same time to teach the child the concept of jumping and the verb to jump, which she uses as if it were a noun, a thing, just like in the naming game. In order to teach the concept of jumping, the mother turns it into a thing and she shows the child 'jumping' just as she would show a robin or a fire-engine. In this way, she is explicitly teaching language.

The framing of language should continue in school. Looking at language is an important part of children's understanding of their social and cultural environment. As the Kingman Report (DES 1988) commented:

> It is just as important to teach about our language environment as about our physical environment, or about the structure of the English language as about the structure of the atom. (p. 4, para. 12)

Further, developing an understanding and appreciation of language forms and functions encourages a greater cultural awareness, an awareness of processes of social change and of how people work with and through language. The report *All Our Futures: Creativity, Culture and Education*, published by the National Advisory Committee on Creative and Cultural Education (DfEE 1999), stresses the need for children to 'understand and respect different cultural values and traditions and the processes of cultural change and development'. It prioritises creative thought and action as the means by which such knowledge will be brought about. Language is a focus for and a means by which such creative thought and action can be developed.

SUMMARY

In summary, there are three main types of knowledge about language:

- Implicit knowledge which all speakers of a language possess. Families and schools nurture implicit knowledge as the child's competence grows. Implicit knowledge can be about the forms and the functions of language.
- Explicit knowledge of the functions of language, what language can do, how it is used and for what purposes.
- Explicit knowledge of the forms and structures of language. This includes grammatical knowledge and the terminology necessary for describing and discussing the forms.

Provision needs to be made for each of these types of knowledge.

Next we need to recognise some principles relating to the approach to teaching children about language:

- The major resource for learning about language is language in use, the language that children see, hear and experience all around them. Textbooks alone can't provide this. Children need opportunities to investigate language, actively to find out about it, in the world around them and, most importantly, in the literature they read.
- Productive and engaged responses are important in the study of language. This means that children need to have opportunities to use language in creative ways, to respond in creative ways to it. Filling in gaps in exercises does not provide this.
- Opportunities for talking about and studying language need to be ensured. These can occur in the normal, everyday work of the classroom – we need to be alert to such opportunities and to exploit them. I call these incidental opportunities. But there is a need to provide also for more focused and sustained attention to language, to set up activities, projects, sessions, where language is the central purpose. Language must take its place as part of the content of the English curriculum, beyond the confines of the literacy hour.

- An educational model of language, particularly in the primary years, must be eclectic. It will need to call on a range of linguistic disciplines, including:

phonetics: the study of human speech sounds
semantics: the study of the meanings of words
grammar: including syntax (the structure of sentences and texts) and morphology (the study of word forms)
discourse analysis: the study of spoken interactions, which includes pragmatics (the study of the purposes language is put to)
sociolinguistics: the study of language from a sociological perspective
psycholinguistics: the study of language from a psychological perspective.

Whether we are discussing dialects in the school neighbourhood, or examining the different meanings created by moving a comma, these disciplines provide the broad context in which we are working, the visible part of the linguistic iceberg.

We need to create a classroom climate where language matters, where talking about language is a normal part of the life of the classroom. Whatever the outcomes of the current controversies about the teaching of language, and it is likely that there will always be such debates, the development of children's interest in and knowledge of language, alongside their ability to use it, must be an objective of the language curriculum. Children need the skills to create and participate in language events in the many forms in which they will encounter them. The creation of a 'community of enquiry' (Prentice 1991) will ensure this.

HOW DOES THE NLS RELATE TO THESE PRINCIPLES?

The NLS directs teachers to pay systematic, focused attention to language during the literacy hour. This attention has three orientations: at the level of the word, the sentence and the text. The Framework describes the process of reading a text as involving the use of a range of searchlights, or strategies, to get at the meaning of the text. These strategies are the informing principle underpinning the NLS and are defined as:

phonic (sounds and spelling)
grammatical knowledge
knowledge of context
word recognition and graphic knowledge.

The searchlights are used to seek out meaning and in learning to read, we are told, the reader will use all these strategies, though the balance between them will vary according to the stage of learning the child is going through. Fluent readers use all of them unconsciously, whereas beginning readers may rely more on one than another. The literacy hour takes each of these strategies and provides activities at a group and individual level which will develop children's literacy.

The metaphor of the searchlight is interesting: searchlights try to find something, to catch their target in their beam, to identify it and fix it. There is no reciprocity between searcher and sought, no sense that the searchlight might influence or shape what it finds. This may seem rather an abstruse argument, but I raise it because the metaphor suggests a way of looking at reading as a passive activity, where meaning resides in the text and must be winkled out (another interesting metaphor!) by the reader, as distinct from one in which meaning is actively made by the reader bringing knowledge, experience and understanding to the text.

The key to success will be the extent to which teachers can keep sight of the whole within so many parts. The NLS prescribes targets for each term of a child's primary schooling, it partitions reading into sets of skills and could be interpreted as mechanistic in approach. The challenge is to recognise individual needs in reading development, since not all children will progress at the same rate, nor will they necessarily need exactly the same strategies.

So children will be exposed to activities and discussion which will enhance their understanding of written language: however, it must be stressed that the main purpose of the NLS is to develop competence in literacy, rather than to study language as such. The Framework identifies that literate primary children should have an interest in words and their meanings, and that they should have 'a suitable technical vocabulary through which to understand and discuss their reading and writing', (p. 3) but it must be remembered that the strategy is not the whole English curriculum and there is much that the strategy cannot legitimately deliver. Learning about how spoken and written language is used in a wide range of contexts involves and includes more than is covered in the NLS: the issue is whether schools are in fact spending any time on English beyond the literacy hour. Of particular concern is the development of speaking and listening, which receive a cursory reference in the Framework, but which are not a feature of the strategy. Cordon (2000) argues strongly for an incorporation of interactive dialogue into strategies for literacy development and more considered attention to this a key aspect of learning.

Chapter 2

Spoken language and written language

The problem is that children write the way they speak.

This chapter considers whether there is any truth in this commonsense assertion. We look at the characteristic features of written and spoken language and at the implications of their similarities and differences for children's developing competence in literacy.

Writing and speaking are different from reading and listening because they are productive forms of language. Reading and listening are certainly active, but clearly of a different order from writing and speech. Speech comes before writing. Children learn to speak before they learn to write (though the two do begin to work in tandem very quickly) and most of us use much more spoken language than written language in our daily lives. There are languages which have spoken, but not written forms, but, apart from artificial languages created for particular purposes, it is highly unlikely that a language could exist only in the written form.

Linguists must use as their data the language people speak. They have mapped the spoken languages of the world, divined their grammars and lexicons. However, traditionally linguists have studied speech in an abstract form, rather than analysing the actual utterances of speakers with their hesitations, interactions, intentions – all the messiness of human linguistic interaction. It is only relatively recently that transcripts of actual spoken language have been used in published texts, rather than sentences created by the writer to demonstrate a grammatical point. It is relatively recent also that a focus on functional linguistics and on the sociolinguistic aspect of the discipline has emerged. Writing has received less attention from linguists; in fact, a very influential linguist, Leonard Bloomfield, argued in 1935 that writing was not language but 'merely a way of recording language by means of visible marks' (p. 21).

As a counter to this, Perera (1990) argues that 'writing is not merely a way of recording speech, a kind of inefficient tape-recorder, but a different form of language in its own right, which can lead to different ways of thinking (p. 232).

In a language which has no written form, all the required functions of that culture can be met through speech, otherwise a written mode would emerge. In a society with both modes, the needs of the society are fulfilled through both modes, with some needs being more appropriate for speech and some more appropriate for writing. As Halliday (1985) argues:

> They are both forms of a language; it is the same linguistic system underlying both. But they exploit different features of the system, and gain their power in different ways. The idea that spoken language is formless, confined to short bursts, lacking in logical structure, etc. is a myth – and a pernicious one at that, since it prevents us from recognising its critical role in learning. (p. 100)

Although within the discipline of linguistics spoken language may be prioritised and given higher status than writing, written language has come to have immense prestige in popular perceptions and in education. Spoken language is often judged against the grammar of written language and found wanting. Writing is considered to be the proper form and it follows that speech is a debased version of writing. Criticisms about standards in language, referred to earlier, work on the assumption that the way people speak is deteriorating all the time, and that this is adversely affecting standards in writing. Writing appears to be more stable, and therefore more trustworthy, than speech, because changes in language happen more quickly in speech.

It is important from an educational perspective to clarify this muddle. Speech and writing are separate and different forms of language, requiring different kinds of orientations. At a basic level, spontaneous speech is interactive, face to face, involves at least one other person and is context dependent in that the context is evident and need not be explained. Writers do not have this interactive or reciprocal context: they do not have to negotiate turn-taking or have physical access to the people they are communicating with. They do have to be more explicit and to call on a different set of strategies.

I use the term 'spontaneous speech' because it is necessary to differentiate kinds of speech and kinds of writing. Some speech is more like writing, for example, a lecture or a prepared political speech. Some writing is more like speech, for example, personal letters and messages. Although there are many grammatical and lexical differences between speech and writing, there are many contexts in which the two come together. Rather than thinking of language as either writing or speech, it may be more helpful to see that there are language forms which are more speech-like and others which are more writing-like. This would then account for the examples given above: a personal letter has the cadence of informal speech; it is not the same as the writing in a formal business letter. The terms 'speech' and 'writing' differentiate the mode but not the style of the language.

Both speech and writing happen in a context and the creation of spoken discourse or a written text is determined by choices made from the language system. These choices have to take into account the intended or actual audience, the purpose and content, and the forms available. This sounds rather complex, and it is. Put simply, writers and speakers do not operate in a vacuum: what they say and write, and how they say and write it, require linguistic choices and are influenced by the culture in which they are operating.

HOW IS SPEECH FORMED?

Speech is sound and sound is formed by pushing air out of the lungs, through the nose or mouth. On this journey air is made into sound by the organs of articulation, which include the lips, teeth and, very importantly, the tongue. The study of the sounds of a language is called phonetics.

Vowel sounds are made by unimpeded air shaped to make a particular sound and with sound from the vocal chords which vibrate. The sounds of consonants are made by impeding the air flow. Some sounds are **voiced**, which means the vocal chords give a sound to them, such as the *b* sound in *bond*. Others are **unvoiced**, such as the *p* sound in *pond*. Other examples of voiced and unvoiced sounds are *this* and *thistle*, *laze* and *lace*, *very* and *ferry*.

Vowel sounds emerge as one sound only, but there are sounds which begin as one sound and are changed to a second. These are called **diphthongs**, or **vowel glides**, and are present in words like *loud, soil, fade*. If you say the vowel sound slowly you will feel the shift. This sound is made irrespective of the actual number of vowels in the syllable. **Triphthongs**, as we might expect, have three sounds in the syllable, and are less frequent, occurring in words like *fire* or *our*. The final vowel sound is called the **neutral vowel**, or **schwa**. This is the most common sound in English, but it does not have an alphabetic letter to represent it. It is found at the end of *father, sister*, at the beginning of *another*. However, if the speaker uses a rhotic dialect, which means pronouncing the *r* sound after vowels (now lost in **Received Pronunciation** (RP)) then the neutral vowel is not heard. **Rhoticity** is evident in many accents of English, but these tend to have a low status: in the United states, the reverse is the case, for example in New York.

Some consonantal sounds are **plosives**, or **stop consonants**, which means the air bursts out past the lips, like *p* and *b*, *t*, *d* and *c* and *g*. If you hold your hand up to your mouth, you will feel the air coming out. Some sounds are **fricatives**, which means that air is forced through constricted lips, causing friction, as in the word fricative itself, where the teeth and lips touch and air is forced out through the constriction. Some are **nasal**, which means that the uvula (the small fleshy projection hanging from the back of the mouth above the throat) closes and the sound comes through the nose instead of the mouth. This is evident in words with *m* and *n* sounds, like *mother*, which is **bilabial** (putting the lips together) and *nothing*, which is **alveolar** (using the tongue against the hard palate, near the ridge of the teeth), and also at the end of *sing*, where in RP this sound ends in a soft, not a hard *g*. This is called a **velar nasal** sound and it can only occur in English at the end of a word. Elocution teachers through the ages have tried to teach their students to use it and to eradicate the hard *g* in words like *dancing* because they used RP as the norm for pronunciation. Words ending in 'ing' are very interesting from the point of view of pronunciation, because they are often pronounced *in*, so *goin* instead of *going*; such pronunciation is often labelled as 'dropping your g's'. This is an example of a common misunderstanding which assumes that spelling is more significant than pronunciation. In fact, ironically, the dropping of the final *g* sound used to be an indicator of upper class speech, captured in expressions like *huntin'*, *shootin'* and *fishin'*. Whatever our own views on this, we do need to recognise that the pronunciations I have referred to above are not universal pronunciations for all English speakers.

It is also important to recognise that there are many more sounds in English than letters of the alphabet. This is where a purely phonic approach to learning the alphabet and learning to read is inadequate. For example, the letter *l*, is pronounced differently depending on the word it is used in, such as at the beginning of *like* and at the end of *dull*. This difference is between a *dark l* and a *clear l* and to form the difference the tongue is placed in a different position in the mouth.

So spoken language involves the production of sound. The actual sounds produced will be determined by the geographical region and social group the speakers belong to, that is, their dialect and accent. Linguists make no value judgements of these, but attitudes to people's dialects and accents permeate social life in Britain. The dialect with most prestige is that of Standard English, though, interestingly, RP does not share the same high status. Research by Giles (1971) showed that respondents did not trust speakers with RP. When responses to RP speakers were elicited, respondents considered them favourably in terms of their competence, confidence and determination, but less so in terms of their personal integrity and social attractiveness. It is interesting to speculate about whether there has been a significant change in attitudes since the early 1970s. It is the case, though, that certain accents have social connotations which are enhanced by the media, television in particular. A quick scan of accents used on TV indicates the extent to which these attitudes have become embedded: slickness and streetwise qualities are rarely assigned to characters with rural accents.

A MODEL OF COMMUNICATION

Speech is produced by an **addresser** to an **addressee**. A traditional model explains communication in terms of a message being created by the addresser, encoded in words, received by the addressee and then decoded – a kind of telegraphic process. This is presented as unproblematic. I say something to you and you get precisely what I mean. Indeed, sometimes this will be the case: 'Please bring me the dictionary' seems fairly clear and unambiguous, but this clarity exists largely on the page. When uttered, a whole series of possible nuances of meaning and intention emerge, so that it could be said in anger about a dispute over the meaning of a word, just as the speaker is about to prove a point. Misunderstandings do occur, meanings are not always clear, inferences are not neutral, intentions are misread. Language can mean more than it actually, literally says. 'Why do we need to go to your mother's?' contains a whole raft of potential meanings. For example:

- I don't want to go.
- Is there a particular reason why we must go which I need to know about so that I don't put my foot in it?
- I resent always having to go to your mother's on a Sunday.
- We have enough to do without wasting time on this.

Depending on the intonation, the question could be about *why* we need to go, why *we* need to go, why we *need* to go, why we need to go to *your* mother's and so on. How do we ever make sense of all this? We use the context, which includes our knowledge of the situation, its history, each other, the action referred to, and we use our understanding of language conventions.

Pragmatics is the study of the intentions and effects of language, the use of language in context. It tends to focus on short exchanges; **discourse analysis** is concerned with longer stretches of language. One of the most significant aspects of pragmatics is the theory of **speech acts**, which arose from the work of the philosopher J. L. Austin, largely in his influential book *How to Do Things with Words* (1962). Pragmatics deals with relationships and the performance of language (in Chomsky's use of the term), rather than the underlying competence of the speaker. Pragmatics analyses how people use language to mean and do things. When we say something we are doing more than simply creating speech: we actually do things with words – establish and maintain relationships, express concern, lie, charm, argue, persuade and so on. Leech (1983) suggests that using language is a kind of problem-solving activity, where the speakers ask themselves how best to accomplish their aims in the communication and the hearers ask what the speaker means. The telegraphic model of communication referred to above is totally inadequate to account for all that happens when people talk to each other.

Searle's (1969) theory proposes that utterances have force and that we can consider three different aspects of spoken language:

locution: the actual words spoken. Someone performs the act of saying something.
illocution: the force of the words, the effect intended by the speaker.
perlocution: the effect on the hearer. An effect is achieved.

An example may help here. If I am sitting in a cold room and someone enters and I say 'Were you born in a barn?', the locution is the words spoken; the illocution draws attention to the fact that someone has left the door open and it's cold/draughty/a waste of heat. The perlocutionary force, if I've got my message across, is that someone will go back and close the door. We can, of course, choose not to read the utterance as it was intended: I had a friend at school who would reply 'Yes thank you' to questions such as 'Do you have a pen?' Our friendship did not last long.

When language conveys a meaning beyond or in addition to the actual, literal meaning of the words uttered, this is called **implicature**. An amusing example is given by Thomas (1995), in this extract from a newspaper report of a court case:

> At this interruption Mr Findlay for the prosecution asked Churchill if he was denying that he had deliberately set his dog on Police Constable Lloyd. 'Yes, sir,' replied the defendant, 'I do deny it. When PC Lloyd walked into the club, I just said "Oh look, Rambo, a copper" and the dog sort of made up his own mind.' (p. 83)

So words mean more than their literal meanings. We can speak euphemistically, obliquely, ironically: these are obvious examples of the multiple meanings of language.

Some forms of language have formulaic or ritual perlocutionary force. For example:

- I promise to pay the bearer on demand.
- You are sentenced to six months in prison.
- I name this ship.
- I resign.

Searle called these performatives – the verb carries out the force. Often performatives have an effect in law. Obviously, certain conditions must be met for these effects to be carried out. Actors who marry on stage and say *I thee wed* are not actually to be counted as married, and I cannot make you go to prison simply by pronouncing sentence. The conditions necessary are called **felicity conditions**, which means that the participants in the speech act must consent to its effects, the person uttering the language must have the power to carry out the force, and the place in which this all takes place must be deemed appropriate. All procedures in the event must be carried out correctly.

Thomas (1995) cites an interesting case regarding felicity conditions reported in *The Guardian* in 1987.

> A terrible tangle has arisen in Pakistan over a local soap opera. Soap star Uzman Pirzada divorced his television wife in traditional Muslim style, pronouncing Talaq – I divorce thee – three times. The trouble was that his TV spouse was played by his real wife, Samina. Now the ulemas are saying that the divorce is binding, even though the formula was spoken in the interests of art. Their decree maintains that the Prophet ordained that in three matters (marriage, divorce, the freeing of slaves) words uttered unintentionally or even in jest cannot be withdrawn. Divorced they are and divorced they must remain. (p. 43)

Between the intention of the speaker, and the actual effect of the speech, there is room for multiple miscommunications and misunderstandings. To this picture of the complexity of communication, we need to add a number of other issues.

Linguists have suggested that a principle of *politeness* permeates all spoken communication. Most speakers are concerned to be polite, though one must recognise that this belief is very culturally specific and that politeness is not demonstrated in the same way or held in the same esteem by all cultures. Lakoff (1973) proposed three maxims in relation to politeness:

- speakers try not to impose on the people they are speaking to;
- speakers offer options to the hearer so that the request seems less manipulative or demanding;
- speakers try to make the hearer feel good.

People assume that these maxims are being followed by the people they are communicating with. When they are ignored, or flouted, the nature of the interaction is changed and we are forced to think again about what is going on.

There are many ways in which these maxims can be achieved. We make apologies for asking for things. If we need to borrow a lawnmower, we do not march round to the neighbours and say 'Please lend me the mower'. Even the use of 'please' does not make this more acceptable. We are more likely to say 'Sorry to trouble you but I was wondering if I might borrow the mower again. Ours will be fixed soon, but not until next weekend'. This example shows also how we give options: it allows for a negative response ('Sorry, we've taken it in for a service'). The apologetic style often expects a negative response: 'I don't suppose you could get the washing in for me?' Of course it does depend on the context. Speakers may also praise their addressees, what is often referred to as buttering someone up so that they will agree to what the speaker wants, though I'm not sure that 'You're really good at getting the washing in' would work as an incentive. Speakers may indicate overt deference to the hearer, or **hedge** to make themselves seem non-threatening. Hedges are manners of speech which we use to avoid getting to the point, like 'er', or 'perhaps'.

All these strategies relate to the notion of **face** – an individual's self-image. All speakers are projecting an image of themselves, and this image can be positively and negatively affected by linguistic interaction. Principles of politeness oil the wheels of communication and enable participants to save or keep face. As well as being polite (usually), speakers wish to cooperate. Here we turn to the work of Grice (1975), who proposed four maxims:

- *Quality.* We usually assume that a speaker is being truthful and accurate in what they are saying.
- *Relevance.* We expect a speaker to keep to the point and not to give unnecessary or irrelevant information.
- *Quantity.* We expect a speaker to be brief and not to construct elaborate monologues.
- *Manner.* We expect a speaker to be as clear as possible.

I'm sure that we all know people who knowingly and unknowingly flout these conventions. There is a notable tension too, between cooperative and politeness principles: how do you tell the truth if it is impolite, as in 'You look awful in that suit'? They are, of course, not meant to be rules for conversation, or treated as formal structures to be learned. They are tendencies noted by linguists analysing spoken discourse.

Another feature of spoken discourse is the way it overtly fulfils Halliday's interpersonal function of language. Some language serves the purpose of binding members of social groups, maintaining relationships. Comments about the weather is a typical British example. No one is actually very interested in the weather, but we exchange comments about it because there is a cultural imperative to do so. Linguists call this kind of language use **phatic communion**, a term coined by the anthropologist Malinowski. Any language forms which reinforce the relationships of the participants come under this definition, as do expressions such as 'Do you get what I mean?' or 'Do you see?', where the speaker is checking the effectiveness of the communication.

The nature of any discourse is determined by the context. Linguists have studied discourse in contexts as different as schools, doctors' offices and courts of law, but context here does not refer only to the setting. In any context there are relationships between people, which may be significant because of their power or lack of power. Who can speak, how and for how long will to a large extent be determined by the relative power of the participants. For example, in the analysis of classroom discourse, most questions are asked by teachers, and the nature of the questions they ask is very different from the kinds of questions children encounter in their out-of-school lives. Children rarely hear *closed* questions outside school. Closed questions are those where a particular answer is expected and are the opposite of *open* questions, where the answer is not pre-determined: 'Who wrote *Charlie and the Chocolate Factory?*' is a closed question, whereas 'What did you think of the story?' is, or may be, an open one. Similarly, the amount of time participants are allowed to contribute is of interest. For example, research by Gordon Wells in the 1980s showed that the difference between home and school uses of language was very marked for children beginning school whose language development he followed from their first words to the end of primary school (Bristol Project). This large-scale project was made possible because advanced recording methods allowed the researchers to capture spoken language by attaching microphones to the children.

Wells found that children at home made nearly three times as many utterances to an adult as at school; that they made nearly twice as many speaking turns in conversation with adults at home; that they expressed twice as many different types of meaning at home than at school; that they initiated three times as many conversations at home; that they asked three times as many questions at home; and that adults asked many more questions and made many more requests in school than the children experienced at home. The statistical evidence shows that children have to learn to operate in a very different linguistic environment when they go to school, and one which may not be as beneficial to their overall language development.

In school children were initiating less, speaking less and expressing fewer meanings than they were at home. This may be understandable in the context of a busy classroom with thirty children, but it may also be something we should be concerned about. The evidence that children have to learn new ways of using language and interacting through language in school arises from linguistic analysis: discourse analysis, such as counting turns in a conversation, can provide valuable evidence of the way language is used in the classroom and it can enable teachers to understand more about the role they have and how they might change the way things are done.

One important aspect of discourse analysis is **turn-taking**. In formal settings, such as meetings, there are codes of behaviour which participants usually, though not always, respect, such as the oddly phrased 'speaking through the chair'. Even where participants do not conform willingly to this practice, it is a procedure to which the chair of a meeting can turn if chaos reigns and the meeting becomes a free-for-all.

Sometimes the general script of the exchange requires certain patterns of interaction, as in a job interview. In ordinary, everyday conversation, speakers must negotiate turns as they go along, a complex procedure which can go wrong and lead to break-downs in communication, such as the problems caused when people do not wait for a turn but speak over the end of someone's utterances, or when people finish what other people are saying for them, though such behaviour can, in some contexts, be seen as cooperative rather than offensive, particularly in single-sex, same status conversation.

Conversation progresses through a system of **adjacency pairs**, a term used for exchanges where one utterance expects another utterance in response. An offer can be accepted or refused, but for it to be ignored altogether would be problematic for the speaker, unless such a non-response were seen as a rejection. Questions usually elicit answers, greetings usually require a similar response. A response which is the most common one, that is, the most often given, is called the **preferred response**, and one which is not expected is called the **dispreferred response**, for example:

> You will be coming to the pub tonight, won't you?
> Well actually, no.

Speakers get their turn by using various strategies which happen in milliseconds, including:

- eye contact: listeners tend to look at the speaker if they want to be next to speak;
- intonation: a downward intonation may indicate that the speaker is finishing and act as a cue to the listener to come in;
- tags: speakers can signal an ending by using tags such as 'isn't it?' or 'do you see?', thereby enabling the turn to be handed over;

- syntax: knowledge of syntax enables listeners to recognise points at which an intervention can be made: for example, when a clause is completed and before a new one is begun.

Children learn turn-taking before they can actually produce recognisable speech, because adults model conversations with them, leaving gaps for responses and themselves providing the preferred response. These patterns of engagement are not culturally universal and there has been much research to demonstrate this, particularly in relation to gendered ways of talking. Coates (1989), for example, argues that women have very different conversational styles from men; and research into language in the classroom through, for example, the National Oracy Project, shows significant differences in the way girls and boys learn through language and learn to use language. Perhaps some of the most influential findings from research into discourse practices relate to turn-taking between teachers and children, and the orchestration of language in the classroom, an issue to which we now turn.

DISCOURSE ANALYSIS IN THE CLASSROOM

Sinclair and Coulthard (1975) created a scheme for analysing classroom discourse which has been highly influential. They showed that the linguistic organisation of teacher-child interactions (actually they focused on secondary pupils) reflected the social order of their roles and that the talk in any classroom can be defined according to a number of categories which relate to the function of the language. They analysed the exchanges between teachers and pupils and proposed three categories for the structure of these exchanges:

- *initiation:* the teacher asks a question that invites a response: 'What kind of leaf do you think this is?';
- *response:* the child answers or responds in other ways: 'An oak leaf';
- *feedback:* the teacher evaluates what the child has said: 'Yes, well done'.

Discourse analysis seemed to provide a rigour which had been lacking in educational research, and it was taken up with enthusiasm in the applied context of the classroom. Sinclair and Coulthard, it must be noted, were not educationalists but linguists who had chosen the classroom as the site for their research. The exchange structure came to be known as Initiation, Response, Feedback, or I–R–F. However, the research was more concerned with participants' roles and functions than their intentions or meanings, and it depended on the researcher's interpretation and understanding of what was being said. As we have seen, the interpretation of meaning is not straightforward. An example of this in discourse analysis is that anything the teacher said after a child's utterance was noted as feedback, when in fact it would have been possible to see it as a response to the child's contribution. So although the I–R–F framework has been useful in demonstrating the power relations and formulaic patterns often evident in classrooms, it does not provide a sufficiently honed theory for learning.

Other significant contributions to an understanding of classroom discourse have come from the work of Edwards and Mercer, published in *Common Knowledge: The Development of Understanding in the Classroom* (1987). As the title suggests, they looked at the creation of common knowledge between children and teachers, at how knowledge is jointly constructed, and at the role of context in learning. They proposed that the approach to learning adopted by a teacher, largely through language, creates two different forms of knowledge: ritual knowledge and principled knowledge. They suggest that ritual knowledge is where the children acquire a procedural, 'right answer' orientated competence, whereas principled knowledge is explanation orientated, that is, principles are embedded, understanding is more complete. Ritual knowledge, they claim, arises from the ground rules for discourse, which orientate children to come up with a right answer, having read the cues given by the teacher.

These cues drive the exchanges between teacher and children. In establishing and maintaining control of the learning that takes place, teachers use a range of strategies, both consciously and unconsciously:

* They indicate what is or is not significant through strategies such as *ignoring a contribution:* the class learns that this means the contribution is illegitimate.
* *Re-wording* the children's contributions and recapping what the children should have done or understood, using the voice to highlight important parts of what they are saying, by for example, slowing down or speeding up, speaking loudly or softly.
* *Creating formulaic expressions and sayings* to capture what it is that is being learned: in the example given by Edwards and Mercer, the teacher had created the rhyme 'The shorter the string, the faster the swing', in a lesson about pendulums. This functioned as a shared marker of knowledge.
* They create a context of joint, shared learning in the classroom, through speaking at the same time as the children, or by using *we*. In this way, the children are given the impression that their knowledge and the teacher's knowledge are little different: we are all learning this together.
* They elicit contributions from the children by patterning the exchanges so that an expected answer emerges, or by indicating with their tone of voice which is a preferred answer, or by giving big hints about the desired response. Cued elicitiation (giving children cues to say what you expect them to say) can be achieved also through gesture and eye contact and is a very common teaching strategy in situations where teachers feel their role is to draw out the child's knowledge through a kind of Socratic dialogue.

WHAT WRITERS DO

We have looked at some of the main features of spoken language, from the production of sound to the analysis of discourse. Children have also to learn the practice of writing: what is it necessary to deal with when moving from the spoken to the written mode? A closer look at features of written language will enable us to make comparisons with spoken language and to understand something of what children have to learn in order to become effective writers.

Firstly, and obviously, writing happens mostly in the absence of the reader or intended audience. It does not involve face-to-face contact and is therefore less context dependent than speech. There will be kinds of writing which do rely on the context, such as labels, or instructions for assembling furniture, but on the whole writing is more free-standing. It assumes an absent reader and this implied reader needs the writer to be explicit. The implied reader has a very significant influence on the writer, firstly in terms of the writer's general intentions toward the reader, that is, that the writer has a kind of reader in mind and will select what to write accordingly. Secondly, the reader's needs will usually be taken into account by the writer. The text will be organised for ease of reading and the writer will need to ask 'What does the reader need to know here?'

Explicitness is achieved in a number of ways: for example, by reducing the number of elliptical references. **Ellipsis** is the term for things missed out of sentences because they are already known or given. The gap is filled by referring to what has already gone.

Where are the car keys?
On the kitchen table.

It is unnecessary to repeat 'the car keys are', or even to use a pronoun like 'they'. The speakers understand each other perfectly well without having to be explicit. We do this very often in speech: imagine what conversation would sound like if we had to include everything, every time, in a literal way. But in writing, ellipsis is less frequent. There are also fewer **deictic references** in writing. Deictics are words which refer to specific things without naming them, like pointing in language and they include **demonstratives**, words like *this, that, here, there, these, those,* and personal pronouns such as *his, her, mine.* Speakers use them a good deal because the thing referred to is obvious to the participants in the speech: '*this* wallet', 'you need to go *that* way', 'come over *here*'. In writing, what is referred to must usually be stated and made known.

Whereas speakers can check that they have been understood and they can fill gaps or add more information ('I forgot to mention'), writers have to predict reader's responses and have to take more care over the ordering of the ideas and information. Writers manipulate the syntax of sentences to create the emphasis they need. For example, they can move important information to the beginning of the sentence, or make sentences passive. One would expect that any information in the wrong place, or omitted, would be rectified at the editing stage.

Without face-to-face communication, **paralinguistic** features are not possible. These are non-grammatical means by which the speaker signals importance, such as gesture, intonation, stress, volume and so on. In writing, these have to be achieved by other means: punctuation, type face, grammatical constructions that create emphasis, such as placing the words in the **theme** position in the sentence, so that it is foregrounded. Theme is a linguistic category which means the first part of an utterance, the element we read first. It need not be the subject of the sentence, but because it comes first, it is highlighted and carries the weight of the meaning of the sentence. The rest of the information in the sentence is called the **rheme**.

WRITING AND ITS FORMS

The basic unit of speech is the **clause**, and of writing, the **sentence**. Or to be more precise: 'speech, typically, consists of chains of coordinated, weakly subordinated and adjoining clauses; writing, by contrast, is marked by full subordination and embedding' (Kress 1982, p. 31).
There are four kinds of sentence:

- **declaratives** are statements
- **interrogatives** are questions
- **imperatives** are commands
- **exclamatory** sentences are exclamations.

There are four kinds of clauses:

- *Independent clauses:* A clause makes a sentence in its own right, making sense on its own: 'I ran for the bus'. This is also a simple sentence.
- *Coordinated clauses:* Two clauses are joined together and the clauses are of equal importance: 'I ran for the bus and dropped my purse in the road'. Two clauses are linked together with the conjunction *and*. Any other conjunction can be used.
- *Main clauses:* Main clauses are defined by their relationship to another subordinate clause. So instead of coordinating, there is a relation of subordination involved.
- *Subordinate clauses:* These are dependent on main clauses for their meaning: they cannot stand alone: 'I ran for the bus just as the heavens opened'. The main clause here is *I ran for the bus; just as the heavens opened* is a subordinate clause. It would not make sense to say or write only 'just as the heavens opened'. It is incomplete. Of course one can think of occasions when, for example, it would be used as an elliptical answer:

When did you go shopping?
Just as the heavens opened.

However, from a grammatical point of view, 'just as the heavens opened' is an adverbial clause of time because it answers the question 'when?'. Other possible adverbial clauses are:

  — *manner:* How something is done: I ran for the bus *as though my life depended on it.*
  — *place:* Where something is done: I caught a bus *where the London Road joins the High Street.*
  — *reason:* Why something is done: I caught the bus *because I was too tired to walk all the way home.*

Coordinated and subordinated clauses create complex sentences. In summary, a clause can be a sentence in its own right, but if all written language consisted of single independent clauses it would make reading very taxing. The ability to handle subordination and coordination is one sign of maturity as a writer, though by no means the only sign. In speech, anything goes and clauses can be strung together with 'ands', without anyone really minding.

LEXICAL DENSITY

Writing tends to be more lexically dense than speech. **Lexical density** is a way of describing how 'heavy' a piece of language is, and in order to understand this concept we need first to look at **lexical words** and **grammatical words**.

Lexical words are words that have content: they represent things. Grammatical words have functions but they do not really mean anything independently. Halliday (1985) suggests that grammatical items belong to closed sets, whereas lexical words belong to open sets.

> For example, the personal pronoun *him* contrasts on one dimension with *he, his;* on another dimension with *me, you, her, it, us, them, one;* but that is all. There are no more items in these classes and we cannot add any. With a lexical item, however, we cannot close off its class membership; it enters into an open set, which is indefinitely extendable. So the word *door* is in contrast with *gate* and *screen;* also with *window, wall, floor* and *ceiling;* with *knob, handle, panel* and *sill* . . . there is no way of closing off the sets of items that it is related to, and new items can always come into the picture. (p. 63)

Grammatical words include prepositions, conjunctions, modal verbs (have, will, should, etc.), articles and some adverbs.

The following example compares a piece of writing and a piece of spoken language. They are fairly typical of their mode and are analysed in terms of the number of lexical and grammatical words they contain:

> The question of language and its political implications has exercised writers, philosophers and social theorists throughout the intellectual history of western civilisation. (Cameron 1985)

lexical words: 13; *grammatical words:* 9

> It was a really hot day and so we took a picnic to the park.

lexical words: 5; *grammatical words:* 10

There are of course grey areas about whether a word counts as lexical or grammatical, (for example, some adverbs do and some don't) and it has been suggested by some linguists that it is more appropriate to use the unit of the clause to work out lexical density, rather than the total number of words in the sentence or utterance. However, the purpose of such analysis is to show that writing tends to be more lexically dense. The index of this is a ratio of lexical items to the total number of words in the sample. In the first example, the total is 22 and the ratio is 13 to 22, or 59 per cent, or 0.59. In the second, the total is 15, the ratio is 5 to 15, or 33 per cent, or 0.33. The higher the lexical density, the further from speech the text is considered to be.

Writing tends to contain more **passive** than **active** verb constructions. *The children broke the window* is active. The subject comes before the verb. *The window was broken by the children* is passive. The order of the sentence is changed so that the object of the verb is put in the theme position. Passive constructions mean that the writer can choose whether or not to include the **agent** of the verb, the thing or person that does the verb. We could in this case leave out any reference to the children and say: *The window was broken*, thus removing the agency. The passive form minimises reference to people as agents and for this reason is often found in formal texts.: *London was chosen as the venue for the event*: but by whom?

Expanded noun phrases also make a text feel 'heavy'. Put simply, these are phrases that contain nouns and have the grammatical status of nouns. For example, I can expand *car* into *the pale green car parked outside the supermarket*, thus making an expanded noun phrase. In this case, *car* is known as the **headword**. I can make this phrase into a sentence by adding a finite verb: *the pale green car parked outside the supermarket was clamped*. Expanded noun phrases are more typical of writing than speech because a speaker is not likely to overload the listener with so much condensed information.

Because speech is not usually planned, it is characterised by a high level of **redundancy**. The fillers, hesitations and repetitions of speech pad out the actual message, so that in terms of conveying that message, much of what is said is redundant. This is not to say that these hesitations and so on are irrelevant: they are essential to the interaction; they establish and reflect the tenor of the interaction, the relationships of the participants and the attitude of the speaker to the content. They also contribute to politeness principles (don't impose) and to turn-taking arrangements: if a speaker finishes a turn with a flourish, we may feel that they have finished, but drifting off into another *err* means that they may have more to say. Examples of very low redundancy in written language can be found in newspaper headlines and on occasion this can have startling and unintended results: *General MacArthur flies back to front*.

One of the reasons for the higher lexical density of writing is its tendency to use **nominalisation**. This, in its simplest form refers to the way processes are turned into things. Perera (1984) gives this example:

The extension of fishing limits by Iceland and other countries has meant that Fleetwood's traditional Distant Water fishing grounds have been closed to its trawlers.

The underlined words form an expanded noun phrase, a phrase that is a thing. It is the subject of the verb *has meant*. It could be replaced by a noun, for example:

This dispute has meant that Fleetwood's . . .

which shows that it is acting as a noun. Compare it with this version which Perera suggests is more like spoken language:

Iceland and other countries have extended their fishing limits and this has meant that Fleetwood's traditional Distant Water fishing grounds have been closed to its trawlers.

Here the underlined words are a clause (there is a verb, *have extended*), not a phrase, and a process rather than a thing, is described. Incidentally, this example also supports the argument that spoken language is less lexically dense: nominalisation contributes to lexical density and is unusual in speech.

COHESION

Because writers have to be more explicit than speakers, they have to ensure that a text is coherent, that all the links are made so that it hangs together. A series of unconnected sentences would not necessarily constitute a text. For example:

We went out into the garden. The hospital visiting hours were very limited. Angus made himself a whisky soda.

Again it may be possible to make coherent sense of this, and it is astonishing how readers do strive to make sense of what they read and to tolerate uncertainty and lack of clarity, but it is unsatisfactory as a text because there are no links from sentence to sentence. Readers expect that the content of a text will be consistent and that the ideas, concepts and events in the text will be related to each other. This operates at the text level as well as in relation to inter-sentential linkage. For example, the novel *Watership Down* would be very strange with a chapter on the breeding habits of rabbits in the middle of it, though it is important to note that postmodern writing exploits such readerly expectations.

The grammatical linking or structuring of a text is called **cohesion** and this is a very important aspect of writing. Cohesion is an extensive and complex system of relationships through which langauge binds into a coherent whole. The most obvious form of cohesion is the use of overt linking words like *however, therefore, consequently, first, next*. These explicitly mark connections in the text, usually in relation to the flow of ideas.

From a grammatical perspective, the most common forms of cohesion are **reference** and **substitution**. Consider: *The dinner was ready. It was curry* *again*. Here, the noun *dinner* is not repeated in the second sentence: a **pro-form** is used in its place, in this case a pronoun. This serves to link the two sentences, to show their relation to each other. This is called a cohesive tie and in this case it is **anaphoric**, that is, a backwards tie, because the tie relates to something already established. *It* refers to *dinner*. Ties can also work **cataphorically**, or forwards, with the pro-form first, followed by the noun, as in this example: *In a report <u>she</u> prepared in 1996, and which has subsequently been implemented by all the relevant committees, <u>the Leader of the Council</u> proposed radical changes to the terms of reference of the council's committees.* Here *she* looks ahead to the name of the Leader of the Council. However, this structure must be used with care, because too long a gap can be confusing or irritating for the reader.

Possessive pronouns can also be used cohesively: *She was looking for a hat for the wedding and I told her she could borrow mine* (*mine* and *hat* are related).

Substitution is the use of expressions like *the same* or *so* or *one* to replace words or phrases as in: *I thought the idea would work but he didn't think so* (*so* represents *the idea would work*). *It was an old sweater, one my sister had given to me* (*one* represents *an old sweater*).

These are all examples of grammatical cohesion, that is, cohesion which works through the grammatical relationships of words. A second kind of cohesion is achieved through semantic cohesion. This refers to the way vocabulary holds the text together, as words associate, group together or relate to each other. The use of **synonyms** is an example of this, where words of similar or related meaning are used to avoid repetition: *She drove through the rain to the psychiatrist's. This shrink was costing her a fortune* (*psychiatrist* and *shrink* are synonymous).

Hyponyms work similarly to relate items of vocabulary. An example would be *potato, parsnip* and *cabbage*, which are all hyponyms of *vegetable*. We call *vegetable* the *superordinate* and the relationship of the items is that items belong to the same category, all coming under the superordinate term. For example: *She needed a new uniform for school, so her mother bought a blazer, tie and shirt in the regulation colours* (*blazer, tie* and *shirt* are hyponyms of *uniform*).

Long texts achieve their coherence through the use of these and other forms of cohesion.

SPELLING

Writers need to be able to spell. As children move from the oral to the written mode, they have to rely less on the sounds of words and more on their visual form. The traditional approach to the teaching of spelling, that of sounding out, requires the translation of a visual sign, the word, into sound units which are then encoded into visual form again. This is a difficult task. English spelling is not entirely phonetic and this strategy will only work for some words. Teachers need to recognise which words do have a direct sound-symbol correspondence, requiring a description based on **morpho-phonemic** relations, that is, the relation of sound to morphemes, or parts of words. The words are spelled as they are for historical or etymological reasons. The stories behind some irregular spellings may help children to remember the spelling: for example, *ghost* was originally *gost*, but when Caxton began to print, he used European compositors, (many from Holland) and they wrongly used the *gh* common in Dutch for the spelling of this word.

Gentry (1982) suggests five stages in spelling development. These are not absolutely discrete categories: a writer could be using a mix of strategies from the stages and individuals will develop abilities within stages at different rates. Nevertheless, Gentry's research proposes that they are recognisable stages through which children develop their ability to spell. Gentry's stages are:

- *Pre-communicative:* the child understands that writing makes meaning and knows some letters of the alphabet, but some will be invented or will be numbers or pictures or even musical notes where the child has encountered these!
- *Semi-phonetic:* the child is beginning to show an awareness of letter-sound correspondence and may use the name of the letter as its sound.
- *Phonetic:* the child uses largely a sound-symbol basis for spelling, with some more visual letter strings (common letter patterns) evident and a few common words correctly spelled.
- *Transitional:* here the child is developing a visual memory and relying on it more in spelling. Letter strings are more accurate and more words are correctly spelled and sounding out is relied on less.
- *Correct:* here the child is operating largely correctly, able to use a range of strategies, but more dependent on visual ones, understands many aspects of spelling such as spelling rules and patterns.

As children develop as writers, they have to learn to use their visual memories of written language, to draw on their reading and their own previous writing in order to build up a bank of automatic spellings and ways of working out spellings for new or tricky words.

PUNCTUATION

Writing requires punctuation to mark boundaries and status. In speech this is achieved through intonation, prosody, paralinguistic features and so on, though this is not to suggest that punctuation mirrors intonation in speech. They are two separate systems with some interrelations.

Punctuation is necessary for two reasons. Firstly, it marks boundaries between units of language – phrases, clauses and sentences. Secondly, punctuation marks status. Is the sentence a statement or a question? Is a character shouting? Is it direct speech? So in approaching the teaching of punctuation we need to be clear about these two functions. We also need to recognise that there are two main aspects of punctuation: rules which must be used and conventions which are more open to interpretation. Examples of rules in English are:

- capital letters at the beginning of sentences;
- full stops to end sentences;
- question marks at the end of sentences which are questions;
- apostrophes to mark **elision** (don't) and possession (John's) (*its* is the possessive exception).

Other aspects come under the heading of stylistic or rhetorial usage, where personal preferences or the need for a particular emphasis may dictate the punctuation. The rhetorical aspects of punctuation achieve effects of attitude, tone, emphasis. They operate as conventions rather than rules and their use is much less prescribed: commas, colons, semi-colons, exclamation marks, brackets, dashes, etc. For example, punctuation can be used to constrain the possible meaning of a sentence:

The boy *who fitted the description* was taken in for questioning.
The boy, *who fitted the description*, was taken in for questioning.

The punctuation changes the meaning here: in the first, *who fitted the description* defines the boy, whereas in the second it is a secondary piece of information and the main focus (clause) is *the boy was taken in for questioning*. This demonstrates that punctuation is not secondary to the writing process, but integral to the making of meaning.

GENRE

Genre is an important aspect of the relation of spoken and written language. The term may be familiar from a high culture perspective, where it refers to categories such as film, novel, poem, or at a more specific level, to the characteristics of particular kinds of novel or film such as horror or comedy. In relation to language, different types of writing are described as belonging to different genres, as are different types of spoken discourse: for example, sermons, interviews, political speeches. Genre analysis involves the detailed consideration of the structures of text types, of the larger scale structures beyond the sentence. In this sense, it marks a distinct break from some practices in the teaching of writing which focus on smaller units of language and rarely consider anything beyond the sentence. This is not to suggest that smaller units of language are entirely excluded from this theory of teaching writing: attention is given to forms of language within the sentence but in relation to the whole.

The argument is that different kinds of genres are more or less powerful and give different access to social and political power. In order to be empowered, children need to be able to write the powerful genres. In this way they will gain more control over, and be able to effect change in, their lives.

In developing as writers, children need experience of reading and writing a range of types of writing, or diatypes. Whereas in the past HMI reports have pointed out that primary practice tended to prioritise the narrative genre over all others (for example, the 1989 HMI report on the teaching of reading), the National Curriculum in England and Wales and the NLS require that children must have experience of a wide range of text types: scientific reports, diaries, novels, brochures, etc., thereby gaining a broader experience of generic forms. This is a significant development in primary practice, and beneficial provided that children are able to develop an understanding of the contexts in which the texts are used in addition to the linguistic characteristics of the texts. Genres are structured ways of organising language with some predictability and consistency. They are social constructs, in that there is no linguistic reason why an experiment cannot be reported in the form of a rap, but there are social conventions which determine that this is not the norm. Children need to understand this.

A number of questions arise in relation to the teaching of genres:

- Which genres should be taught?
- How many are there and which are most appropriate in an educational context?
- What aspects of the genre should we be teaching?
- How linguistic should we get?
- Once we have decided how linguistic the teaching should be, how do we actually teach children to write the genre?
- Which methods and practices are most appropriate?

Which genres?

Discussions about genres usually begin with the question of definitions.

People in every culture develop characteristically patterned ways of using their language. Becoming literate in the culture involves being able to use the language practices of the culture, to be able to read and write the texts the culture creates. As part of being literate, we learn how and when to use certain language forms, and the genre is the socially recognised form through which the social situations and relations are conducted. Genre involves not only the medium (mode) of the text, such as a letter, or a novel, or a till receipt: it includes the tenor, the relationships between reader and writer. Writers need to handle this essential aspect of communication.

Writers can, of course, write anything they like, but usually they are not starting from scratch in deciding how to shape a piece of writing. Constraints and conventions operate which writers can choose to use or to reject. If I want to leave a message for the milkman, I am not particularly troubled by how to do this. But what if I chose to write it like this?

1, High Street,
Newtown,
Anyshire

The Milkman,
Milko Dairies, Newtown,

Dear Sir,
Further to my request of last week, I would be grateful if, with immediate effect, you would make an alteration to the regular order I hold with your company and supply an additional pint of milk until further notice.
Yours faithfully,

What are the linguistic conventions being flouted here? The level of formality is an obvious one, and the vocabulary is therefore not appropriate to the social activity of ordering milk. This is not an efficient way of achieving what I want. From the reader's point of view there are expectations too, and the milkman would no doubt be rather surprised to receive this. We do not have to come up with our own way of doing things every time we write, because to do so would be very inefficient, though in fact in this example, I have used an inappropriate genre rather than creating my own. It is worth noting, however, that the chances are that I would get my milk. What would be in question would be the social relation between the participants in this event: he would think I was pretentious. However, if the context, for example, were changing an order for double glazing then this style of writing might be more appropriate than a casual note. Unless children have an awareness of the conventions, they will not be in a position to write against them, or to adapt them to their own needs.

How do we decide which genres to teach? This is more a social and political question than a pedagogic one. Genre theorists, as linguists who argue strongly for a genre-based approach to writing have come to be known, have proposed that **expository** writing is more important socially than narrative. Exposition is mainly factual and is conducted through more impersonal language: it can involve explanations, reasoning, examples, the development of argument. Genre theorists argue that exposition is more powerful than narrative: it is the language which is used in public discourse and contrasts in this sense with narrative. Although narrative may be a necessary starting point for children's journeys as writers, genre theorists argue that an approach to writing which allows narrative to be the main genre and which allows children to write about subjects in their own words, will not do. In fact, Martin *et al.* (1987) talk of children being 'stranded' in what they term child-centred practices, that is allowing the child to write anything, in any way. They claim that a genre-based approach, which foregrounds certain kinds of expository writing, will empower the writer and that if children do not learn to write the genres necessary in a world of information-processing and technology, their participation in that world will be impaired.

There is no definitive list of all known genres and their structures: such a taxonomy is probably an impossibililty – the list would never be completed. Social and cultural practices change, writing changes. We are doing different kinds of writing today from those of even twenty years ago. Genres gradually fall out of use, or the social relations embedded in a genre shift, making new demands on the genre form, as a historical comparison of formal business letters shows. Now that electronic communication is embedded in the culture, new forms and styles of writing are emerging. This form of communication has moved from the public to the private domain very rapidly and as a result, older genres are gradually being lost. In addition, the Internet has introduced new genres, new styles of writing, widening the range of text types which children encounter and need to be able to read and write. Something as common as the instruction booklet for a mobile phone poses new challenges for the reader.

How linguistic?

Genre theory becomes more contentious when the question of the actual linguistic structures of texts is addressed. A further reason why a taxonomy of genres is impossible arises from the problems of actual classification. There is a debate about whether, beyond a few major categories, it is possible to fit all texts into a finite number of categories. Many genres are blends of other genres. Different parameters will render different groupings and the extreme case would be that there are as many genres as texts.

If it were possible to show that texts within a given genre have similar structural features, which then become their defining feature, then this suggests that any example of a given genre will be identical in structure to any other example of the same genre. All newspaper editiorials would have the same shape and use the same linguistic structures. This is clearly not the case in practice, though it can be seen that there are similarities in purpose and style. This suggests that texts may share some similarities in their structures and linguistic choices, but that these are not hard and fast and cannot be treated as templates which writers impose.

Take, for example, a type of writing the genre theorists call **report** writing. This involves a description; the language is **non-chronological** (not time orientated). Reports are contrasted with **recounts**, which are chronologically organised, as in: *We went to the zoo and we saw an elephant.* Reports provide a body of information which has to be ordered, and the genre theorists present models for this organisation. For example, a piece of writing about mammals would have:

a general opening classification: basically what mammals are;
a description of appearance: what mammals look like;
a description of habits/behaviours: what mammals do;
a closing statement.

At a more detailed level, teachers would be encouraged to teach the children about some or all of the following features of this genre:

- The kinds of verbs that might be in a text like this. For example, in reports we might find the simple present, or universal present tense: *owls eat, dolphins live, soil provides.*
- The use of generic participants or subjects. We might find reference to *the heart* or *dinosaurs*, but not perhaps to a particular heart or dinosaur.
- The lack of temporal sequences, that is, those to do with time. There are usually no chronological stages to the processes described (no *and thens*, for example).
- The use of clauses using the verbs *to be* and *to do.*
- The use of agentless, passive verbs, such as *mammals are found*: no one or thing does the verb, therefore it has no agent. The alternative might be to say *you can find mammals*, but genre theorists would argue that this is the wrong kind of tone for a report.

This does rather seem like teaching an approved formula, and it is difficult to see how this helps children to engage in a genre which exists in the world, unless the children are going to be entry writers for encyclopoedias. It is not the kind of writing which helps children to engage with social processes in their lives. In fact, this kind of writing is a highly school-orientated one and its applicability elsewhere must be rather limited. At one time it might have been possible to say that this type of text could be found in information books and text books, but publishers today produce information books which are exciting, innovatory in style, raising further questions about the rigidity. Are the children learning about mammals through the writing, or presenting their knowledge about mammals for assessment by the teacher? In other words, is writing a process of engagement with an aspect of learning, or a product? Is there a relationship between constructing a text in this way and learning about the topic being written about? Who is the audience for such writing? What happens to personal, individual knowledge a child may have of the topic: must this be left out? These are important questions.

Teaching written genres

The Cox Report (DES 1989) identified five purposes for English in the curriculum. Briefly, these are:

- for personal growth;
- for adult needs;
- for cross-curricula learning;
- for the development of knowledge of the cultural heritage;
- for the development of cultural analysis.

This way of looking at English generated much debate when the National Curriculum was first exposed to public scrutiny. The purposes Cox posited are largely self-explanatory and, as is the danger with any such categorisation, are not intended to be interpreted as discrete categories, since the English curriculum will develop all of them in varying ways and at various times in a child's experience of schooling. It is a question of balance and weighting. The teaching of written genres relates particularly to the first three purposes, though knowledge of textual structures and purposes can certainly enhance understanding of the literary and cultural heritage of English and can contribute importantly to the development of critical literacy.

One of the main criticisms of genre theory arises in relation to the tension between personal growth and the needs of the adult world. For example, children's writing is often criticised by genre theorists for not conforming to the linguistic structures of an implied target genre, an adult genre.

Kress (1982) analyses a number of child texts for their approximation to the adult form of the genre. He states that expository writing, such as reports, encode a view of knowledge as a timeless universal, in which all sense of the self should be completely negated, and all the attention of the writer should be focused on what is being written about, its properties and features. According to Kress, a child who writes of the beaked whale:

> The beaked whales live out in mid-ocean, where the tasty squid are found...generally members of this family have long, narrow snouts, or beaks...it is unusual in colour, so if you should see one, you should be able to recognise it (my editing),

has not quite grasped the genre because of the use of *you*, which is too personal: such direct appeals to a reader are seen as breaking the generic structure.

This is a good example of the tension because it assumes that interactional references like this are not acceptable, yet such styles are evident in many information books for children. Indeed, one might argue that this demonstrates a response to the role of writer and an excellent recognition of the need to engage an audience. It is also possible that this serves as a reinforcing strategy for the child's own knowledge: she is talking to herself as much as to her reader.

Similarly, Barrs (1995) has commented on the analysis of children's texts by Rothery and cites the following example as evidence of a rigidity in attitude and lack of understanding of children's purposes.

> I sor a bike in the shop.
> My dad woot by me the bike.
> After school sar a big box in my bed room.
> A bike.

Rothery comments that the last line is inappropriate in writing and should be expanded to *It was a bike!* This comment does seem to indicate a lack of understanding about what the child is trying to do: the sentence is effective as it stands. It would be necessary to know more about what was to happen to the little story before commenting on the need for greater linguistic explicitness.

Children have needs as writers, and to use adult genres as target texts and to assess children's writing in the primary years against those texts, is to ignore their needs now, to neglect the personal growth aspect of writing and the purposes writing serves for children in their development as writers. Many genres that children use are transitional, part of the process of coming to understand a more recognisable genre, but these are often judged as failures.

This is not to suggest that genre theory is irrelevant to the needs of primary children. It is necessary for children to understand some of the typical features of some texts, to learn to write them and adapt them to their needs. This is part of what being a writer entails: to reflect on language in use. It is a question of degree, choosing the appropriate context in which to teach aspects of genre and using this approach as a complement to a wider approach to writing, based on developing a sense of audience and purpose in writing.

Children do not learn to write different genres only by osmosis, that is, by absorbing a model provided by the reading of particular texts, although this is an essential part of the process. They need support in reading the unfamiliar genre, discussing its features, writing drafts, and finally, explaining in a more explicit way, what they have done. It is now taken for granted that children will need scaffolded support in learning to write for a variety of purposes, but there is less consensus as to how this should be done. A pedagogical process for this might include:

- *Immersion:* For example, if the new genre is a procedural text, such as a recipe, a range of recipe books should be in the classroom to be read, discussed and used.
- *Identification of generic features:* for example, enlarged texts can be provided so that children can work out together what some of the generic features are.
- *Modelling:* Children should jointly, then perhaps individually, follow a recipe and make something, with the emphasis being on whether the recipe's instructions actually work. If the children think the recipe doesn't give enough explanation of what to do, an adapted recipe could be produced. Activities can then be developed to focus on the features of the genre, in this case, for example, the use of imperative verbs such as *beat, place, put, line, bake, mix,* or the structural organisation of the text into sections, such as a list of ingredients and a method. The children could be given a recipe with the imperative verbs removed and could either provide their own verbs in the blanks or use the list provided by the teacher. Recipes could be sequenced, to reinforce their procedural nature.
- *Independent construction:* The children begin to write their own recipes. They can be provided with a list of ingredients to use to create a dish, or a photograph of a dish to be made, or could write a recipe for a really horrible dish or a magic spell dish.
- *Reflection:* This is a very necessary stage in the whole process, because it gives children the opportunity to explain what they have understood and what the typical features of the genre are.

The process from dependence to independence through scaffolded stages of support by the teacher is reflected in the orientation of the literacy hour.

Clarkson and Stansfield (1992) give a good example of this process in practice in writing recipes for pizza with a Year 3 class. Cambourne and Brown (1989) suggest a more developed model for learning new genres, though the principal features are the same.

WRITING FRAMES

Teaching approaches which offer children structured support for the shaping and construction of different text types are now becoming quite well developed and are referred to in the NLS. Writing frames enable children to organise their writing, and therefore their thinking. They are outlines, skeletal structures which can be created to provide a great deal, or very little, guidance to the writer. Frames help cohesion, they can give connectives to link the stages of the text, which can range from linking words such as *often, then, usually, sometimes, afterwards, firstly, nevertheless, although,* to more extended phrases for inter-sentential linkage such as *and as a result, so now you can see why, the chief reason is.* One key issue is the point at which this scaffold is withdrawn. As Costidell and Lewis (2000) point out: 'pupils can continue to use a writing frame until they feel able to apply their knowledge of the genre they are working with and decide on their own way of organising the material and their own connective phrases' (p. 26). This transition may be more difficult than is suggested and we need some evidence of the extent to which children who have been taught to write using frames can be creative and reinterpret them. A further concern is for any templates to be contextualised in a learning context. They need to arise from a real purpose and not be an end in themselves: as Lewis and Wray (1995) point out, 'the frame itself is never a reason for writing' (p. 60). This is a very important point: frames are not formulae, though there can be a strong temptation to treat them as such. Riley and Reedy (2000) argue that frames can be used with very young children and give persuasive examples of this, from procedural texts to argument, from recounts to narrative. It is even more important that frames are used with sensitivity in the early years of learning to write.

The grand claim made for genre theory, that it empowers writers, has been challenged by many teachers and researchers. The gist of opposing views is twofold. Firstly, the argument is that social empowerment will not come about simply through learning to write in certain sorts of ways; social empowerment will depend on the kinds of social organisations and communities a person belongs to. Secondly, writing can only be effective if it has an effect on someone reading it, which must be the primary aim of teaching writing. Writing to a formula will not bring this about. Nevertheless, more directed attention to text structures and organising features can help children to organise their thinking in and through written language.

In summary, the teaching of generic features in the later primary years will be beneficial if the overall approach recognises the needs of the developing writer through:

- differentiating the process of writing from the need for a final product for assessment;
- developing the interactive, dialogic processes of writing;
- engaging with purposeful writing activities;
- accepting the concept of a *transitional* genre, which may not resemble an adult text but which serves a very important learning function;
- recognising that being able to handle the social transaction function of genres requires attention to the notion of an audience or a reader.

IMPLICATIONS FOR CHILDREN'S WRITING

Differences between spoken and written language mean that in learning to write, children must adjust to the conventions of a different medium. Writing requires a great deal more than putting words together with punctuation. What kind of help do children need in developing control of this medium?

- Be positive in responding to their work. Not all the errors children make in writing are negative: often they are evidence of trying out new forms and testing knowledge about language. If children are afraid of making errors, they will never improve. Taking risks is an important aspect of development in writing.
- Not all strengths in writing are visible. The forms children have rejected, such as the exclusion of more typically spoken forms, are not always easy to infer. This is why monitoring their writing over a period of time is better than treating each piece of writing as a perfect, finished form, representing what the child can do at this point in time. The teacher's record of the child's growth will include tracking of more complex grammatical features.
- Children need to know what kind of text they are writing, which means in turn that they need to have read, discussed, modelled and experimented with a range of genres. The teacher needs to be explicit and clear about the kind of writing expected: 'write a story' may mean write a report, or an account, and these are important distinctions for the writer. The children need to consider the following questions.

Who is this writing for?

Note here that audience encompasses real and implied readers. It also requires a consideration of relationship, or tenor, between the writer and the reader. The way you write to someone you know well is different from the way you would write if you did not know them. The handling of these levels of formality, which are aspects of the register of the text, is evidence of increasing maturity in writing.

What is the purpose of the writing?

This includes a consideration of the role of language, whether it is to persuade, make an argument, describe, report and so on, and how best to achieve the purpose.

What form should the writing take?

This requires consideration by the writer about what forms are available and how to choose among them. Children should have experience of making such choices, but rarely do, since it is usually the teacher who sets the writing task and prescribes its form. By the end of the primary years, children should have had opportunities to discuss and justify genre choices, as a step toward greater autonomy in their writing.

The writing repertoire needs to be broad, which means that the reading repertoire must be too. The inclusion of non-fiction texts in the reading box or corner will enable children to read beyond narrative forms. This category includes newspapers, magazines, brochures, pamphlets, encyclopedias, dictionaries and adult information books to supplement the usual information books available in the classroom.

Children need to hear the language of non-fiction, so it is important to read this aloud to them, just as one would fiction. The benefits are similar: children get to hear language which may be more complex than they can cope with in reading independently and they will absorb some of the structures and features of written language.

Children need help at the level of the sentence in their writing so that they can learn what the possibilities of the sentence are and how this is different in writing from speech. At primary level, we can't expect children to have a thorough understanding of these grammatical points, but I would argue that there are some aspects that we should introduce through discussion of their work. Here are some examples.

Recognising a phrase and a clause

Usually a phrase does not contain a verb whereas a clause does. This is a basic distinction although there are such things as verbless clauses. However, for the purposes of helping children to construct sentences, this is broadly the case. Sometimes a word can seem like a verb but isn't: for example, *realising my mistake* is a phrase, not a clause. This is an important distinction because a common error is to present a phrase as a sentence, even in adult writing.

> Going down to the coast last week.
> To pick your own strawberries.
> Finished her chapter yesterday.

These are not clauses and cannot stand alone as sentences. They use the **non-finite** form of the verb.

The main verb in a sentence must be finite. Again one must add the caveat that this is usually the case, because there are many examples of published works where in fact this is not the case. For a verb to be finite, it must mark **tense**. If we look, for example, at the verb *to skip*, the inflectional endings which show the tense are skip-*s* and skipp-*ed*. These are the bits added to the stem which indicate present and past tenses. In English, there is no future tense marked in the same way as past and present: we make the future tense by using an auxiliary, such as *will*.

It may be easier for children to understand the difference between a phrase and a clause if they can find the subject and verb in the clause, because these are constitutive of the clause. Once the clause, or section of writing is identified, it facilitates discussion about links. Children can go through their writing and mark the subjects and verbs before discussion with the teacher. It is important to remember that the subject can be a phrase in itself: *that very sad day when my hamster died* (subject) *is* (verb) *etched in my memory.*

Linking clauses

Clauses cannot be linked by commas – another common problem: *we went out last night, my dad bought me fish and chips on the way home, they were great.*

If children can understand the constituents of a sentence, they may be able to identify the problem here. The solution in this example might be to identify the independent clauses which operate as sentences: *We went out last night. My dad bought us fish and chips. They were great.* This is fine for this example, but a whole text written in independent clauses would be very disjointed and unsatisfactory for the reader. Children need to understand how clauses can be coordinated: *We went out last night and my dad bought me fish and chips and they were great.* The problem with simple coordination like this is that, in children's writing, coordination can be used to excess (the 'and and and' text teachers know so well!) so this would need to be monitored. In this example we might want the children to recognise that there could be two coordinated clauses and an independent clause: *We went out last night and my dad bought us fish and chips. They were great.*

Perhaps the most difficult kind of link to manage as a developing writer, possibly because it is very unlike spoken language, is subordination. For example: *When we went out last night my dad bought us fish and chips and they were great.* Discussing examples of subordinated clauses from their reading will provide useful models for the children and their own writing will provide a starting point for learning how to link clauses in these three essential ways.

However, it must be stressed here that although maturity in writing involves the ability to handle complex clause structures and relations, this must follow on from, not precede, an engagement with ideas and the finding of a personal voice in writing.

Punctuation

Punctuation is often conceived as something added on to writing, rather than being part of the grammatical structure. Teachers may encourage children to write and not to worry about the punctuation because that can be put right afterwards. There does come a point, however, when the punctuation needs to be seen as integral to the thought processes being recorded and to their syntactical organisation. It is a matter of using standard punctuation where necessary (the rules) and choosing appropriate punctuation where necessary, according to the effect (the conventions).

The apostrophe is probably the punctuation mark most commented on, as lost, missed and misused apostrophes are hunted down. It may be the case, as some linguists suggest, that since there is usually little problem caused by incorrect use of the apostrophe, it is first in line to disappear: if it is not actually essential to communication, we can probably do without it. A trawl through today's free paper through my door and a Dulux colour chart finds these examples:

OUT OF HOURS HEALTH SERVICES
Would you like to assist your local health authority in finding out more about local peoples priorities in relation to local health services?

Hadley's: Ladies and Gentlemens hairdressing

SIGHTSEEING TOUR OF PARIS . . . visiting the picturesque artist's quarter

Softer Shades of Jade: jade with it's Eastern influence immediately brings an atmosphere of restfulness and relaxation.

And of course there are the ubiquitous examples of greengrocers' abuse of the apostrophe, as in *tomato's and potato's*. I recently saw a very strange new version of this usage in *r'hubarb*. These examples of incorrect uses or omissions of the *apostrophe* do not actually impede meaning, but they do receive a great deal of attention in the complaint tradition. It may help children to understand that the apostrophe *s* to mark possession represents the *es* form of Old English and is attached to the word which indictates possession, which can be singular or plural. Montmartre has never been the *artist's* quarter: who was this artist painting all alone? It is the *artists'* quarter. The basic rules are:

- singular: add *apostrophe s*, e.g. *the hairdresser cut the girl's hair* (one girl);
- plural formed by adding *s*: add apostrophe only, e.g. *the hairdresser cut the girls' hair* (more than one girl);
- plural formed in a different way: add *apostrophe s*, e.g. *the men's room* (not *mens'*);
- of course, *its* is the only exception to this rule.

Children will also need help in deciding what to do with words that already end in *s*, usually names like James. Do you add *apostrophe s* or just the apostrophe? When these questions arise, one has to refer to the pronunciation of the word, so we would have *James's adventures in the peach*. However, this is rather a grey area and purists might demand *James'* in spoken and written forms.

Where the apostrophe is used for elision, children will need help in sorting out what is being shortened, so that *do'nt* does not occur. In whatever way these matters are dealt with by the teacher, there will undoubtedly be a rash of apostrophes throughout the children's work on the principle that if you put them in everywhere, some are bound to be correct!

Spelling

Games like Hangman and Scrabble will help children to become familiar with spellings. If Hangman is played so that each letter in turn must be found, rather than any random letter, this will focus attention on possible letter strings and combinations.

The use of 'Have A Go' or 'Try it out' word books, where children are encouraged to try to spell the word first before asking for help, will enable the teacher to see what strategies the children are using in their spelling, so that particular problems or patterns of mistakes can be picked up. If teachers always provide the spelling, the children are not encouraged to work out how to spell a word using their language knowledge. The practice of read/cover/write/check in learning spellings is widely used in primary schools: some versions add *remember* to the process. Both these practices make the children more active, responsible and independent in learning accurate spellings, rather than the honeypot model, where the teacher is the only one to put words into spelling books and she is surrounded by children all needing a word urgently for their written work. Very often the word is already in the child's word book, which shows how successful this particular strategy is. Many teachers now ask the children to leave a space in their writing, or to draw a line, sometimes called the magic line, to show that they need help with a spelling. This practice prevents complete disruption of their creative processes as they keep stopping for help. Children can be asked to underline words they are not sure of before they pass on their work.

Cohesion

In terms of cohesion, children will need help in organising longer stretches of text so that some of the features of cohesion are used. For example, the use of pro-forms, particularly pronouns to represent nouns: *the man answered the door and the man said...* Is this the same or a different man? The context will determine this, but *he* would indicate that the two men are actually the same. Similarly, the handling of deictic reference and ellipsis will need discussion. Children often use **exophoric** reference, an example of deictic reference (things outside the text), without having made clear what is being referred to. For example, this opening to some writing about making templates: *First we folded it in two, then we cut round the pattern.* It is exophoric because it refers to something that has not yet been established, presumably card or paper.

This example raises an important question about the purpose of children's writing. If the teacher knows what is being referred to, and can make sense of what is written, why draw the child's attention to a problem? Might this not be detrimental to their confidence in writing? It depends how the writing task has been framed. If the purpose of the writing has been made clear, and who will read it, then the teacher will have established the ground rules, as it were, for the work. For example, recording observations from an investigation does not require the same orientation to an audience as writing a brochure about the school.

Handling speech

Children will need help in constructing direct and indirect speech. Direct speech can be identified by asking them to draw circles round the words actually spoken, like a speech bubble, and reading aloud will make direct speech more apparent. Indirect, or reported speech is more difficult because it requires a change of perspective, usually marked in the tense of the verb:

He said 'I am going to Italy this summer' becomes

He said that he was going to Italy this summer or

He said that he is going to Italy this summer or

He said that he was going to Italy that summer.

However, most problems with this arise when children are asked to convert from direct to reported speech as exercises, whereas in their own writing the context and a little bit of discussion may be all that is needed to get this right.

Children can learn a little about the way spoken and written language work by audio-recording some spoken language and transcribing a short extract from it. They could begin by recording a single voice, for example giving instructions about how to play a game, and compare this with a written version. Then they could move on to dialogue. Collaborative group or pair work, such as a problem-solving task, provides very good, if challenging, data. The children can discuss beforehand what they think happens in group work and predict what they might find. How easy do they think it will be to write it down? What is missing when they listen to it after the event? They will need some simple transcription notations, for example:

(9) to represent the number of seconds of pauses/silences

_____ used to show simultaneous speech

bold type to show emphasis

(. . . .) to show indecipherable speech

This activity can also be used to help children to reflect on what makes good group work, and their roles in collaborative work. Who is dominant? Who initiates questions?

Standard English

Children will need help identifying examples of non-Standard English in their writing. Obvious examples are:

- subject/verb agreement: in Standard English, for example, *we were* is necessary, not *we was;*
- the use of double negatives: *I didn't do nothing;*
- dialect words and expressions: for example, *he was right mardy, it was well good.*

This is a highly problematic area, firstly because of the dangers of damaging the self-esteem and confidence of writers if they are told without an explanation that such uses are not allowed, and secondly because there is no agreed definition of what counts as standard, only a few key markers as presented above. We need much more knowledge about the permissable range of variation within the standard. Standard English includes slang and jargon, which many non-linguists find difficult to accept. Stylistic preferences and register differences must be distinguished from grammatical forms.

One of the ways of resolving problems about changing children's language is to talk of adding Standard English to children's repertoires, rather than substituting Standard English for their home dialect. If we can teach children about how and when to use the standard, they will be empowered, able to use different aspects of their linguistic repertoire at appropriate points. It is an entitlement. This seems a liberal approach, and many teachers would argue that this is what they try to do. However, we need to know what the effect on the home dialect is of doing this. When the term *Ms* was introduced into the lexicon it had the effect of changing the nature of the words it joined: *Miss* and *Mrs.* Their meanings altered to accommodate the new term and *Miss* no longer neutrally referred to an unmarried woman, or *Mrs* to a married one. New choices were made available and new meanings became ascribed to old words. In a similar, but much more significant way, the addition of Standard English to a child's repertoire must affect the meaning and status of their first dialect, not only psychologically, but cognitively too. The sense of the self constructed through language is changed. We need research evidence as to how and when people who have changed their dialect in this way use their original dialect. To what extent is the notion of a repertoire possible?

It is important that children understand something of this debate, and certainly that spoken and written language are different in terms of their use of Standard English: in writing, the need for a standard is less controversial. Teachers need to be explicit about why they are changing things that children write (and say): this is a fundamental aspect of children's knowledge about language.

SO DO CHILDREN WRITE THE WAY THEY SPEAK?

This brings us to the question with which we began this chapter. I hope that the preceding discussion has demonstrated that this is not a simple question. Some writing demands to be written in a spoken style. But if we take the criticism to be referring to more *writerly* writing, there is a question to address.

Perera (1990) looked at the writing of children aged 8 to 12 to see whether they were using forms more typical of speech in their writing. Firstly, in order to look for them, she had to identify what these typical features might be:

- the clause initiator *well*, which is very common in speech: *well, I told him it was no use;*
- vague completers: *or something, and all that: I heard a noise: it was a car or something;*
- this and these: *there was this man;*
- recapitulatory pronoun: *my dad he had to empty the bins;*
- like: *it was like a bright light* (This is very common in the speech of adolescents at the time of writing, following an American trend and is used to frame a dramatic moment in a monologue: *So I was like (pause) furious about it);*
- tags: *that was a good trick, that was.*

In fact, Perera found very few of these structures in the samples of writing she assessed. In 48 pieces she found only two incidences. Her argument is that by the age of eight or so, children have a well-developed idea of what can and cannot be put into writing, as a result of their reading and discussion of written texts. Children were editing out of their work constructions more frequent in spoken language and she found that children's writing contained many examples of forms which are never or rarely used in speech but are used in writing. In other words, these young writers were adopting and experimenting with the forms of written language, not unthinkingly pouring speech onto the page. This serves as a reminder that learning to use language is an active process, a process of making meaning, and that this needs to be credited in the developing writer.

Rather than stressing what the children cannot do, we need to recognise that in learning to write they are learning to handle a linguistically complex medium. We need to apply our linguistic knowledge of the features of spoken and written language to the processes children are going through and to their development as writers. Linguistic analysis is a tool for the teacher to work with. It certainly does not tell us everything about becoming a writer, but it is an important aspect of the teacher's own subject knowledge.

PART 2
Language Activities

Chapter 3

Looking at language in children's literature

I once saw a scheme of work for a Year 3 class on the topic of food, in which Roald Dahl's *James and the Giant Peach* was identified as the class reader because it had some tenuous relationship with food. I'm sure that the children loved the book and got a great deal out of reading it, or hearing it read, but I cite this example as evidence of how children's literature, particularly novels, can sometimes be used rather tenuously to tie them in with a topic or project. This may seem innocuous enough, but it rather suggests that the choice of literature for reading to and with children should have thematic relevance as its main criterion and that the quality of literature is secondary to its usefulness and relevance to a class topic. In fact, as the above example might suggest, thematic relevance is often perceived more by the teacher than the children. Selecting literature in this way is quite common practice in primary schools: either the story is related to the project, or the themes and subjects for the project are drawn out of the text. Either way, the potential messages about literature are that it relates to other things, but is not valued in itself, for its insights, the experiences – affective and intellectual – it can give.

Now, having made this criticism, it may appear that I intend to do in this chapter exactly what I am objecting to, because I am proposing the importance of drawing children's attention to the language of literature, to the language used in novels, picture books and poetry, as a way of developing an interest in how language is used and what language is. Literature is rich with potential for looking at language in a wide variety of ways. We can draw children's attention incidentally to aspects of language in the text, or linger and take time to consider these aspects and develop activities from them. We can look at language in a particular book or poem, or at more general issues such as the distinguishing features of certain kinds of poems. But whatever the focus or purpose, response to the experience of reading must be paramount. Never sacrifice a powerful narrative to an interesting point of grammar.

Through literature, children are exposed to 'the different ways the language lets a writer tell and the many and different ways a reader reads' (Meek 1988, p. 21).

This brief quotation conveys both the complexity and the simplicity of the reading process: writers can tell their stories in many ways, through a variety of discourses, and readers make their own sense of what they read. Each belongs to a context which will affect the meanings made on both sides of the text. This is not to suggest that readers can read anything in any way they choose. Writers constrain and direct readers in many different ways. As Nick Jones (1990) argues

> The more open a text, the more it encourages the play of memory or intellect, and liberates or enlarges response. (This is one possible definition of literature.) The more closed a text – the workshop manual, the political interview – the more it aspires to close down interpretations and to constrain response. (p. 163)

Readers can be conscious of the writer's craft, or it can be invisible. I am proposing that there are possibilities for turning a little of what is invisible into areas for discussion and debate, for making writing more available and open to scrutiny with children. I am also suggesting that, regardless of the writer's craft, literature uses language in special ways that deserve attention. If we are to help children to engage fully with what is written, we will need to take opportunities to draw their attention to particular aspects of the language, to take small opportunities to develop an attention to how writers use language and to the resources of written language.

We need also to think much more carefully about developing children's responses through listening and the associated importance of reading aloud to children. It is through hearing text read, and read well, that early interest in written language develops: the performance of text is a crucial skill for teachers to develop.

WHAT IS LITERATURE?

In literature, writers are more likely to use language in a literary way than in other kinds of writing. Is that true? In fact, literary language can crop up anywhere, making it rather dangerous to talk as though it belongs exclusively in what we call 'literature' and as if it is a discrete and unproblematic entity. The very word literature is used in so many ways that I even hesitate to use it as the title for this chapter. We talk of classics in literature, of popular literature, and attached to each are questions of relative value and status. The word literature encompasses Jane Austen and the material British Gas sends to its investors, Benjamin Zephania's oral poetry and the works published in an academic discipline.

So what is literary about language? Carter and Nash (1990) argue that yes/no categories in terms of literary language should be replaced with the notion of a cline of literariness, to allow for certain uses to be marked as more or less literary, and that literariness is something to do with function. In other words, there is no absolute definition of literariness in language: language is deemed to be achieving a literary effect when it is used in particular ways. This means that it is not confined to literature as traditionally defined, but can crop up in advertising, in publicity material, in newspaper headlines and so on. It depends also whether a reader chooses to read something in a literary as opposed to a literal way. A good example of this is travel writing, which demonstrates the difficulty of erecting definitions as barriers. Travel writing is informative, contains facts and details from the real world, and in this sense belongs in a category broadly called non-fiction. Yet, people read it on beaches, plunge into its narrative and bask in the vicarious journey it offers as if it were a fictional narrative. This is readily demonstrated in the question of Bill Bryson's work: which genre does it belong to? Does it matter? The boundaries are not fixed.

So literary language is not the exclusive preserve of novels and poems, and the debate about what literature is may seem rather pointless in relation to working with children in school. I raise the matter here because I believe that attention to language in children's books will make children more aware of and sensitive to language used outside books, language as they experience it in their real world, and that both are very important kinds of knowledge about language. Because of the value we place on it in the primary years, literature would seem a proper and rewarding place to start to look at language.

KINDS OF LITERATURE AND DIATYPIC VARIETY

If we begin with the notion of diatypic variety discussed in Chapter 1, literature is evidence of that variety. I am using the term literature here to mean fiction and poetry, whether written with a child reader in mind or not. This distinction may be one we would wish to discuss with children: the history of publishing for children is quite a short one and it would make an interesting investigation to find out a little bit about the history of children's book publishing, starting with collecting information about the books the children's parents read as children and comparing them with some contemporary texts.

Literature comes in many forms and it is important for children to be able to identify some of them. This will only happen if the range of literature available for individual and whole-class reading is sufficiently varied and includes novels, picture books, fairy tales, short stories, cartoon stories, myths, legends, traditional stories and a wide selection of poetry. Within these broad generic categories, other genres emerge – such as fantasy, horror, humour, mystery, school stories – each of which has its own conventions which can be analysed. The following are some suggestions for working with novels and picture books so that children begin to understand some of these conventions, that is, the conventions of particular genres of narrative.

GENRE ACTIVITIES

Books in the classroom or library can be categorised by the children using sticky labels for particular genres. The class as a whole would decide on possible categories in advance, which might have two orientations: the content of the story and the style or nature of the story, though these are not exclusive categories. Suggestions might be

- *Content:* stories about families/friends/travel and going places/school/mysterious happenings/animals;
- *Style:* funny/sad/informative/moving/romantic/thoughtful.

Book jackets and publishers' blurbs can be scrutinised for evidence of the kind of genre the book belongs to, even before reading has begun. Invite the children to speculate and justify their inferences, then to check if they were correct after reading.

A class reading record by genre can be established, as a wall chart for example, so that the children can see who is reading what kind of book. This would be the focus for class feed-back on their reading and new purchases would need to take into account the need to supplement areas and break into new ones. The chart would list generic categories and the children would enter the titles of books they had read by category.

Children's understanding of genre can be extended to consider the genres of television. A viewing record can be kept for either a week, or a day, where the children record all their viewing and categorise the programmes and films they have listed. Categories might include films, situation comedies, game shows, soaps, news, information programmes such as food programmes. There may then be sub-classifications necessary such as live/prerecorded, films made for television and films made for the cinema. There are useful possibilities for using the data gathered in terms of considering how best to present this information: is a list or a graph best or is there a more effective way of presenting the data?

A FOCUS ON NARRATIVE

To be able to identify different features of narrative texts lays the foundation for a closer attention to narrative itself. What is a narrative? In the field of literary theory the study of narrative is an immensely complex pursuit, encompassing psychoanalysis, linguistics, cultural studies and many other discourses and disciplines. Narrative is described as central to our functioning, to our processing of experience and our expression of that experience. For young children, surrounded from birth by stories, narratives provide a framework through which their own experiences can be understood. Mercer (1995, p. 5) cites a very interesting example of a child using the voice of the storyteller in her own life and the language of story to express her feelings about her own situation. Having asked her father twice to play with her, Anna says 'Daddy! Daddy will you play with me? (pause) She said to her Daddy'. This last sentence re-positions Anna, helping her to frame her experience (being ignored) through a linguistic structure typical of narratives. She is, effectively, commentating on herself, turning herself into a character. Similarly, the child who sorted her toys into piles and then stole them back with the cry *That's a nice doggy: I'll have that,* shows us the power of narrative. *Burglar Bill* by Janet and Allan Ahlberg helps this child to make sense of and act on the world as she knows it: in the story, Bill sees valuables in people's homes and seizes on them with 'I'll 'ave that!'. However, narratives are not confined between the covers of a book, or to the tale told at bedtime. Nor are they simply aesthetic conventions used by writers or choreographers to tell us something. Narratives pervade our consciousness as we process events and their consequences. We tell stories to ourselves and others about our lives; we rehearse scenarios and dialogues we may experience; we recall and reframe things we have experienced and said. As Wells (1986) proposes:

> The reality each one of us inhabits is to a very great extent a distillation of the stories that we have shared: not only the narratives that we have heard and told, read or seen enacted in drama or news on television, but also the anecdotes, explanations and conjectures that are drawn upon in everyday conversation, in our perpetual attempts to understand the world in which we live and our experiences in it. (p. 196)

Toolan (1988) quotes Harris on the displacement elements of narrative (this is the way narratives refer to things which are not there, which have happened or may happen), where he suggests through analogy with the honey bee how uniquely human narratising is: 'Bees do not regale one another with reminiscences of the nectar they found last week, nor discuss together the nectar they may find tomorrow' (p. 5).

Bees can indicate where the pollen is, using reflex actions and instincts to refer to something spatially displaced, but cannot overcome temporal displacement, that is, matters relating to the past or the future. People can do this through language, and narratives are one of the main ways in which this is achieved.

I'm sure that someone somewhere is at this very minute researching into whether narratives are in fact uniquely human: perhaps the most we can say is that humans regularly encounter and create narratives of one kind or another, whether these are oral narratives like anecdotes or jokes, or written narratives of a private or public nature, or thought processes as we rehearse what we will say about why we are so late or why we forgot to buy the milk. For children, narrative provides a powerful introduction to and interpretation of their world. It provides access to worlds beyond their own and experiences they cannot have, and in relation to their development of understanding about language, through reading and hearing narratives children develop an awareness of narrative structures and characteristic features of narratives.

The terms 'narrative' and 'story' tend to be used interchangeably and it may be useful here to make a distinction between them. Story refers to the actual events and actions: narrative refers to the way those events are told, the way they are framed in a text. A narrator will have an attitude to the events and this will be evident in the narrative. In practice in the classroom, this distinction may not be a very useful one, though the term 'narrator' is important and should be introduced.

NARRATIVE IN TRADITIONAL STORIES

Traditional stories, which include fairy and folk tales, provide excellent opportunities for focusing on language and structure. They are short enough to allow comparisons to be made between them, for children to hear or read in one sitting, and they can be selected from a range of cultures. It is important, (and an obvious point) though, that children need to have read a number of stories if they are to make comparisons or to identify typical features. It is also important to note that the activities suggested below are not by any means the only, or main activities one might want to engage in: they are intended to enable a focus on language features, both at a broad structural level and in terms of a focus on the actual words used in the story.

There are many descriptions or grammars of narratives: these are structual analyses which attempt to find and describe what is the same about how narratives work by identifying their main features in terms of events, people and situations. One of the most well-known is Propp's theory of story structure. Propp, a Russian, published *The Morphology of the Folktale* in 1928, in which he propounds a theory about story structure based on his reading of Russian fairy tales. The word **morphology** in his title means the science of forms. Propp was looking at the structural organisation of folktales, and he identified 31 recurring elements or features of the tales he looked at, which he called functions, some of which are recurring, called constants, and some unpredictable, called variables. He argued that although the characters in individual stories might differ, their function in the stories is relatively constant and the sequence in which their functions are fulfilled remains fixed: 'Functions of characters serve as stable, constant elements in a tale, independent of how and by whom they are fulfilled. They constitute the fundamental components in a tale' (1968, p. 21).

ACTIVITIES ABOUT NARRATIVE

Propp's theory is extensive and detailed. In its simplest form it provides an analysis of story structure by identifying what kinds of characters there are and what events they find themselves in. Such comparative analysis can inform children's responses to traditional tales. For example, they can create a list of characters and their different roles in the narrative.

In terms of broader structural analyses, children can be encouraged to identify the sections which constitute the beginning, middle and end stages of stories and to justify their decisions about where one stage ends and another begins. Where there is a main and a subsidiary thread to the story, the terms *plot* and *sub-plot* can be introduced.

Stories can be sequenced. Issue the children with paragraphs or sections randomly ordered from the story so that they can re-construct it from its parts. This example is from *Clever Gretchen and Other Forgotten Folktales*, by Alison Lurie (1980) (Figure 3.1).

In re-creating the original text, children will need to consider such aspects as the *temporal organisation* of the story and links between paragraphs such as *so* and *then*; *language features* such as those typical of beginnings and endings: *there once was*; the *internal cohesion* of the text: for example, the old woman must be established before paragraph 5, where she is referred to as *the* old woman; their *knowledge of the narrative structure*: the parallelism of the good and bad daughters is a structuring device.

The discussion necessary during the task and the reflection after will allow the children to make more explicit the reasons for their decisions about the order of paragraphs. The correct order of the paragraphs in this case is 4, 10, 5, 7, 1, 6, 9, 2, 8, 3, though other patterns are possible and may, in the children's view, be just as satisfactory. Possible configurations should be compared and discussed.

Another activity is to give the children a series of openings for traditional tales and ask them to create the rest of the paragraph. This is not intended as a test of their knowledge of the actual tales, but to enable them to set the scene for a story and to continue in an appropriate style. For example:

> Once upon a time, in the middle of winter, when snowflakes fell like feathers, a certain Queen sat at her window sewing.

> Long, long ago, there lived two brothers. Their father always said what a sharp, sensible lad the elder one was.

> There was once a cook named Grethel, who always dressed herself up very fine and who wore red rosettes on her shoes whenever she went out.

> Many, many years ago there was a terrible drought and all the elephants were desperate for a drink of water.

A similar activity can be done with the endings of stories: the children can either write the whole story which finishes with the sentence or paragraph supplied, or can write a summary of the story. Again, there is no expectation that the children recognise the story. Here is a selection of final sentences:

> Then she spurred her horse and rode off toward her father's castle, where she was welcomed with much joy and feasting.

> Ever since that time the King, as a punishment for his sins, has had to ferry people backwards and forwards across that wide river and some say that he is ferrying them to this day.

> So the young prince was married to his true princess, and when the king grew too old to govern any more, they reigned over the kingdom in peace and happiness for the rest of their lives.

THE BAKER'S DAUGHTER

1 Time went on, and one evening the ill-natured daughter was serving in the baker's shop. The same ragged old woman shuffled in, leaning on her staff, and asked for a piece of dough. The girl grudgingly gave her a small bit, for her father had told her she must be kind to beggars. And might she bake it in the oven? asked the old woman. 'Oh, very well, if you must,' answered the baker's daughter.

2 But when she opened the door again, the old woman's tiny bit of dough had swelled up so much it almost filled the oven and it was all shiny with sugar and full of currants and raisins. 'That's far too large and far too fine for the likes of her,' said the baker's daughter and she put the third loaf aside with the other two.

3 'And so shall it always be for you,' cried the fairy and she threw off her cloak and stood up tall and shining. 'Henceforth you shall say nothing else but *whoo-whoo*.' She struck the baker's daughter with her staff and the girl turned into an owl and flew out hooting into the night.

4 There was once a baker who had two daughters. Though they were twins, yet they were as different as summer and winter. One was generous and good-natured while the other was selfish, greedy, and cross.

5 The old woman sat in the corner and seemed to sleep until the bread was done. 'Wake up, granny,' said the girl; and then she cried out, 'Why, look! The loaf has doubled in size.'

6 So the old woman sat in the corner and seemed to sleep. When the bread was done, the baker's daughter opened the oven door, and saw that the dough had doubled in size. 'That's too large for the likes of her,' she said, and set the loaf aside for herself. She pulled off another piece of dough half the size of the first, and put it into the oven.

7 'And so shall it always be for you, because of your generous heart,' said the old woman, who was really a fairy in disguise. She threw off her cloak and stood up, all tall and shining, and touched the girl with her staff. And from that day on, every loaf of bread or cake or pie the baker's daughter put into the oven came out twice as large.

8 Now the old woman opened her eyes and sat up and asked if her bread was done.
'It was burnt up in the oven, hoo-hoo' said the girl laughing.
'Is that all you have to say to me?' asked the old woman.
'Hoo-hoo what else should I say?' cried the baker's daughter laughing still.

9 Presently the bread was done, and the baker's daughter opened the oven door and saw that the dough had swelled so that this loaf was twice the size of the first one. 'That's far too large for the likes of her,' she said and set it aside with the other. Then she pulled off a tiny bit of dough hardly as big as her thumb, and shoved it into the oven.

10 On a cold evening when the wind swept the streets like a broom, the good-natured daughter was serving in the baker's shop. A poor, ragged old woman came in, leaning on a staff, and asked if she might have a bit of dough. 'Certainly, granny,' said the girl, and she pulled off a large piece. And might she bake it in the oven? asked the old woman. 'Yes, surely,' said the baker's daughter.

Figure 3.1 The Baker's Daughter: sequencing a text

Read a story to its penultimate paragraph, or an appropriate point in the narrative, and let the children predict an ending. Note all contributions and compare them with the actual ending.

Write a whole-class, collaborative story so that the children can share in the modelling of the stages of the narrative. Discuss the structure together: how does it start? What happens to trigger events at the beginning?

The characteristic features of particular traditional stories can be identified and presented as a table. After reading a story, the elements can be discussed and recorded. These might be the elements of *The Singing Tortoise*, retold by John Yeoman (Gollancz, 1993).

place	kinds of characters	important objects	events	outcomes
a forest	a hunter and a tortoise	a golden harp	telling a secret	death/freedom

Many of the characters in traditional tales have common qualities, often stereotypical character traits, particularly where their function, as villain for example, is more important than their character. The children can make a list of the qualities of characters in particular stories and compare them across stories. To what extent are any of the characteristics common to the stories? Examples of traits would be: rich/poor old/young mean/generous honest/dishonest strong/weak beautiful/ugly superior/humblebrave/fearfulloyal/disloyal.

Discussion of character and stereotype will lead into a consideration of gender roles and the way women and girls are portrayed in the stories. The children can debate whether Lurie (1980) is right when she says:

As for the heroines, things just happen to them: they are persecuted by wicked stepmothers, eaten by wolves, or fall asleep for a hundred years. All most of them do is to wait patiently for the right prince to come, or for someone else to rescue them from dangers and enchantments.

The numbers of male and female characters and their roles in the story (mother, queen, woodcutter, hunter) can be collected and discussed. This could be in relation to one or more stories. Can any patterns be discerned?

Picking out the adjectives and verbs used to describe male and female characters may provide some interesting data: in rereading *Snow White*, I find:

Wicked Queen (adjectives): haughty proud tall jealous beautiful.

Good Queen (verbs): sewed looked (I) wish (baby) born (to her).

The King's son (verbs): hunt rode begged carried answered.

What is the effect of such language choices to depict characters? Note in relation to female characters that verbs are often intransitive, or passive: the queen does not have or deliver a baby, a baby is born to her (passive), and verbs like *look* and *wish* are intransitive because they do not take a direct object. Transitive verbs need an object in order to make sense: *she ordered a Chinese takeaway*, whereas intransitive verbs do not need an object to make sense: *she tires easily*. This is why defining verbs to children as *doing words* is inadequate and often confusing to them, just as saying that nouns are the names of things is inadequate in explaining abstract nouns like *love* and *persuasion*.

Children can compare typical and non-typical features of a story written to be non-sexist and of a traditional one. For example, Grimm's *Sleeping Beauty* can be compared with *The Paperbag Princess* by Robert N. Munsch, which ends rather untypically:

> 'Ronald,' said Elizabeth, 'your clothes are really pretty and your hair is very neat. You look like a real prince, but you are a toad.'

> They didn't get married after all.

A significant feature of traditional tales is reward and punishment of the characters. What are the rewards and punishments in a particular story? Who is rewarded and who punished? Are the rewards and punishments fair or justified? Are there rewards and punishments common to any stories?

Many tales arise from the oral tradition of storytelling and contain linguistic features which contribute to the interactive nature of the telling. The children can analyse what these features are and try to identify features which suggest an implied listener. Often in such stories there are repetitions of phrases or formulaic uses of language, such as wishes or spells, and events will be patterned and repeated in order to help the listener to remember them, in the absence of a written text to which to refer.

A comparison of two different written versions of a story will provide an interesting focus for attention to language and to the intentions of the writer. For example, the 1853 version of Grimm's *Hansel and Gretel*, anthologised by Iona and Peter Opie, can be compared with Anthony Browne's illustrated 1981 version of Eleanor Quarrie's 1949 translation. One obvious difference is the length of the texts, with the earlier text considerably longer than the later. This may have something to do with the status of the illustrations by Browne, which are as important as the words in this picture book. The children could consider how different purposes are served by the illustrations in each text; the modern illustrations are much more integral and convey additional information. The children could discuss the kind of audience each text might have been intended for. The modern story is contemporised: how this is achieved would provide a good discussion activity. The illustrations play the main role in this, but there are interesting changes in language too: compare dwelt/lived; procure/find; simpleton/fool.

Once the children have an understanding of the formula for the tales, they can write to the formula. A challenging constraint is to write their own story in a limited number of words, fitting into the total all the elements identified. Fifty words is very difficult, but one hundred and fifty might be a reasonable target.

The Stinky Cheese Man by Jon Scieszka and Lane Smith subverts in a number of rich and complex ways, both the traditonal fairy tale genre and the nature of the printed book. The stories of Cinderella and Rumpelstiltskin are integrated so that the main characters meet each other. Characters step outside their stories and address each other as though the book is their world: 'Could you please stop talking in upper case letters? It really messes up the page'. The story ends, or so we think, then one of the characters tells us that this was a strategy to trick the giant and that it hasn't really ended. It wasn't the sky that fell on Chicken Little, but the table of contents. Chicken Little admonishes the authors for putting the ISBN on the back cover: 'This is ugly? Who is this ISBN guy?' The book is full of these intertextual references and frequently steps outside the text in this self-referential way. Children can combine stories they know: what if Snow White met Hansel and Gretel? The stock characters can change their characteristics: a kind wolf, a genie who refuses to grant three wishes, a naughty Red Riding Hood (Roald Dahl's poem about her in *Revolting Rhymes* provides an interesting model).

LITERATURE AND DIALECTAL VARIETY

All the activities above are designed to encourage understanding of the nature and structure of narrative, with a focus on traditional tales, and as such are examples of work on diatypic variation. Children's literature also offers a rich resource for looking at dialectal variety, at how people speak in different ways for different purposes, and at how this is represented in written language.

ACTIVITIES LOOKING AT SPOKEN LANGUAGE IN LITERATURE

Writers capture characters' styles of speaking in order to help us to understand and know them better. For example, in Anthony Browne's *A Walk in the Park*, the class differences in two families, the Smith's and the Smythe's, are shown not only in terms of the houses and possessions they own, and in their names, but, on one page, in terms of the way they speak.

'Ere Albert, 'ere Smudge,' yelled Mr Smith. 'Time for 'ome!'

'Come here Victoria, come along Charles,' called Mrs Smythe, 'Time for lunch.'

This representation of accent provides a useful opportunity for discussion about how people speak and why Anthony Browne chose to portray the two characters in this way. How does this make us feel about them? This is one very small example of a speech style: other examples involving features which are dialect features can be an excellent way of introducing children to the differences between dialects, between accents and dialects, and to attitudes to standard and non-standard English. However, it is quite unusual to find examples of dialect in literature for children. A quick trawl through a selection of children's books reveals very few examples. Notable exceptions include *Burglar Bill*, by Janet and Allan Ahlberg, where Bill and Betty say things like:

and these are his own little clothes, what his grandma knit him

I ain't got no husband

I never knowed there was a baby in here

all them things

that give me a fright

Similarly, Colin McNaughton's *Jolly Roger and the Pirates of Abdul the Skinhead* uses wonderfully evocative speech: 'Poor wee scab!...A livin' 'ell. Oooh-aaargh. It ain't right fer a lad t' be brought up s'clean and 'orrible. T'is the only chance they gits afore they grows up inter people!' The strong characterisation through speech, and the wonderful illustrations with speech bubbles, provide opportunities for discussion about how to represent natural speech and why writers tend to choose more standard written English forms, such as those used by Roger, rather than a transliteration of actual speech.

Characteristics of speech are more often portrayed in standard spoken English, through typographic emphasis and the adverbs used to describe speech, like *angrily, softly, gruffly*. Both these stylistic effects can be explored with the children. Over a period of two weeks, ask the children to find examples from their individual reading of words to describe the way someone speaks. Record these on a chart and then categorise them as a whole-class activity. It is likely that most of the words found will be adverbs and this provides a good opportunity to introduce this term and to emphasis that adverbs typically end in *ly*. Another way in which speech is described is through descriptive phrases like *in an angry way*, or *with a shaking voice*. These examples can be used to create new sentences. Finally, another common way of describing a speech style is through the selection of vocabulary which implies speech, such as *whispered, shouted, screamed*. These can be collected both from texts and from the children's general knowledge. This data can be organised by, for example, volume (loud/quiet sounds) or intention (angry/gentle sounds).

Emphasis, volume and questioning are just three of the effects that can be achieved through punctuation. The use of exclamation and question marks can be examined in the text: for example, how would the following passage from *George's Marvellous Medicine* by Roald Dahl be read aloud?

> The next day, George's father came down to breakfast in a state of greater excitement than ever. 'I've been awake all night thinking about it!' he cried.
> 'About what, dad?' George asked him.
> 'About your marvellous medicine, of course! We can't stop now, my boy! We must start making more and more of it at once! More and more and more!'

What difference would it make if the exclamation marks were deleted? This is a useful opportunity to introduce different kinds of sentences: declaratives (statements); interrogatives (questions); imperatives (orders) and exclamatory sentences (emphatic).

Sometimes, capitals are used for emphasis as in this exchange from *The Battle of Bubble and Squeak* by Phillipa Pearce:

'No,' said his mother, 'no, no NO! Not another day in this house, if I can help it! They go!'
'But Mum –'
'THEY GO!'

Sometimes dots are used to represent speech which trails away, or other similar effects. This example, again from *George's Marvellous Medicine*, shows how dots are used to increase the dramatic effect, as George's grandmother, under the influence of the magic medicine, conducts a monologue about her powers, piling fear on fear for George until he flees for his life and slams the kitchen door shut, leaving her in the living room.

'Some of us,' she said, 'have magic powers that can twist the creatures of this earth into wondrous shapes . . . '
A tingle of electricity flashed down the length of George's spine. He began to feel frightened.
'Some of us,' the old woman went on, 'have fire on our tongues and sparks in our bellies and wizardry in the tips of our fingers . . . '
'Some of us know secrets that would make your hair stand straight up on end and your eyes pop out of their sockets . . . '
'We know secrets, my dear, about dark places where dark things live and squirm and slither all over each other . . . '
George made a dive for the door.
'It doesn't matter how far you run,' he heard her saying, 'you won't ever get away . . . '
George ran into the kitchen, slamming the door behind him.

The power of the grandmother's speech renders George a silent participant and the dots make a considerable contribution to her looming presence . . .

The use of bold and italic typeface can also enable the writer to draw attention to particular words or phrases and children can be shown how to produce this effect when they use a word processor for writing stories.

Finally, the sounds and cadences of speech can be captured in onomatopoeic uses of language. Onomatopoeia comes from the Greek *onoma*, name, and *poiein*, to make. It refers to the way words can represent through imitation the sounds they are describing, to reinforce the meaning of the word. The children can suggest spellings for common words and sounds which fall into the category of onomatopoeia, such as *phew, cor, ouch, ooh, wow, er, umm, mmm*, and can discuss these spellings from a phonetic perspective. Why *phew*, and not *few*? Why *ouch* and not *owch*? Which spellings do dictionaries give? New spellings can be created for words deemed necessary for which no spelling currently exists. Words from the list of words which imply speech, suggested above, can be discussed for their onomatopoeic nature, for example, *whisper, yell*.

Literature can provide models for demonstrating the difference between direct and indirect, or reported, speech. This is often assumed to be difficult for children to grasp in their own writing and I think this is because there is very little evidence of indirect speech in children's stories. In direct speech, dialogue is recorded verbatim, as it were, as the very words spoken by the characters. It is the most common form of speech in novels and, in fact, can be a little problematic in terms of deciding who is actually speaking, because the addresser, or speaker, is often implied but not stated in the text. Sometimes the pronouns *he* or *she* are used, but in single sex conversations, this may be of little help. For the speaker to be named at every turn in the discussion would be repetitive and intrusive: it is a feature often seen in reading schemes where it is wrongly assumed that children cannot supply this inferential understanding to the text.

When speakers are not named throughout the dialogue, it means that the reader has to keep up and sometimes to use their knowledge of the characters to infer who is speaking. For young readers, this is difficult enough when only two characters are talking, though they are able to apply their understanding of the rules of turn-taking, that is, that people usually speak one after another in stories (though not in real life!), particularly where the language used invites a formulaic response, such as in adjacency pairs (for example, questions invite answers, greetings expect greetings). Where more than two characters are speaking it can become very confusing. Talking with children about the conventions of punctuating direct speech can help them to understand how to use these in their own writing.

Speech from novels can be used to model the punctuation conventions for speech. This is quite a difficult convention to understand: at its simplest, it involves putting speech marks around the actual words spoken. There are three places where speech can occur in the sentence:

1. First: 'What time is it?' he said.

2. Second: She said, 'It's six o'clock.'.

3. At the beginning and end: 'If you don't hurry up,' he said, 'we will be late.'

There is always a punctuation mark separating the speech from the narrative. It can be a comma, as above, or an exclamation or question mark, in which case, there is still a lower case letter for the resumed narrative because the sentence is not deemed to have ended: *'Don't do that!' he cried.* The speech marks enclose all that is spoken and the punctuation, in this example an exclamation mark.

LOOKING AT FIGURATIVE AND POETIC LANGUAGE

In this section, I want to argue that it is important to introduce children in the primary years to qualities of language which will develop their aesthetic sense and their response to the language of literary texts. The Kingman Report (DES 1988) puts it thus:

Wide reading, and as great an experience as possible of the best imaginative literature, are essential to the full development of an ear for language, and to a full knowledge of the range of possible patterns of thought and feeling made accessible by the power and range of language. (p. 11)

Although this comment invites questions about what exactly is considered to be the best imaginative literature, and who might decide what should be counted in this category, nevertheless, it reminds us of the importance of developing children's responses to and understanding of the nature of language in literature. This response will be achieved particularly through attention to the language and forms of poetry and it is therefore very important that children have the opportunity to read and listen to poetry and to go beyond reading to describing and analysing how language is used for poetic effect.

This is not the place to rehearse in detail the debate about whether children should read and know about more traditional poetry, or whether contemporary poetry for children is more suitable. The debate, in any case, goes beyond poetry to encompass all literature for children. Whatever the choice of material, there will arise opportunities to discuss the poet's facility with language, particular organisations and effects of words and to encourage critical responses. This will not necessarily damage the child's interest in poetry, as some might argue, as long as the enjoyment of words comes before an analysis of their effects. Poems ought not to be used as comprehension exercises, and any activities which are devised should enhance the children's responses to and engagement with the text. Poems can be selected for their unusual or interesting use of language or form.

ACTIVITIES WORKING WITH POETIC AND FIGURATIVE LANGUAGE

In working with poems, children will need to develop a language for talking about the language of poetry. The kinds of terms appropriate to the primary years will include:

rhyme	assonance	rhythm	syllable	verse
alliteration	stress	metaphor	simile	imagery

Poems can be interpreted and performed using the voice and music or percussion, such as a glockenspiel or tambourine. This approach can provide an excellent focus on language and meaning. For example, *The Dance of the Thirteen Skeletons*, by Jack Prelutsky, is a good example of a poem which uses unusual language, including alliterative and onomatopoeic effects, which can be performed in the classroom. For example, the opening verse establishes a wonderfully evocative scene which can be created through orchestrated voices and percussion instruments: 'In a snow-enshrouded graveyard/gripped by winter's bitter chill/not a single soul is stirring/all is silent, all is still/till a distant bell tolls midnight/and the spirits work their will'. Performing the refrain, 'with the click and the clack/and the chitter and the chack/and the clatter and the chatter/of their bare bare bones' can help children to feel alliteration at work in language and provides a model for their own use of sound and image in poetry.

The rhythm too is skilfully created: the children can beat out the syllables to show the rhythm of the lines. It may help to start with words of one, then two syllables to demonstrate this concept. They could identify the syllables in their own names and look for polysyllabic words in a dictionary. It is important to note here that syllables are not the same as morphemes. Morphemes are the parts that words are made from: we combine morphemes to create words. A morpheme can be as small as *apostrophe s ('s)*: for example, in changing *lady* to *lady's*, two morphemes are combined: *lady* and *'s*. A syllable, on the other hand, is a unit of sound: *lady's* has two syllables: *la* and *dy's*.

In looking at narrative genres, I suggested that children might classify the range of narrative texts in the book corner, or class library, so that they come to recognise some of the features of different kinds of narrative writing. A similar approach can be taken to poetry, where children can begin to identify different poetic structures, particularly in relation to creating their own. Children should learn to recognise simple structures like haiku, limerick, ballad and pattern poems, such as acrostics, where each line of the poem begins with the letters of a word read down the page. In their own writing of poems, a formal structure can be very supportive to the young writer. For example, the syllabic constraints of the Japanese haiku (three lines with five, seven and five syllables respectively), can be an interesting challenge. The following two haiku were written by Stephen (10):

Listen to the rain	Apple on a tree
Tap tap on the window pane	It is red and ripe and sweet
With his little stick	Now my hand will take

Cinquains similarly provide a structure: five lines with 2, 4, 6, 8 and 2 syllables respectively. Poems provide plenty of opportunities for looking at rhyme, including alliteration and assonance, which are forms of rhyme. Alliteration is the repetition of consonants at the beginnings of words, and assonance refers to the repetition of vowel sounds. The repetition need not be in consecutive words and both are used for particular effects.

Children can look for examples of rhyme in everyday uses of language, for example, in advertising and shop names: *Beanz Meanz Heinz; Lavazza: Italian for Life; Hair Flair; Crack down on Crime; P Pick up a Penguin*. Which of these relies on assonance and which on alliteration? Advertisements also provide an obvious source of word play: *Do it Maille Way, Curl up and Dye*.

The children can create an alphabet zoo using alliterative animals: five frolicking frogs; six silly sea-lions.

Show the children poems which use rhyme in interesting ways, for example this short poem from *Mother Goose Comes to Cable Street* (Stones and Mann 1980), where internal rhyme is used (internal rhyme is less common than end rhyme). The children can create their own version using this as a model:

> Fire! Fire! said Mrs Dyer;
> Where? Where? said Mrs Dare;
> Up the town, said Mrs Brown;
> Any damage? said Mrs Gamage;
> None at all, said Mrs Hall.

Introduce children to the labelling of lines of poetry as *a, b, c, d* and so on to indicate rhyme. Some simple verses will enable them to see the rhyming arrangement of the poem.

> I have a little brother *a*
> His name is Tiny Tim, *b*
> I put him in the bathtub *c*
> To teach him how to swim. *b*
> He drank up all the water; *d*
> He ate up all the soap; *e*
> He lay down on the bathmat *f*
> Blowing bubbles from his throat. *e*

Rhyming and patterning are combined to great effect in 'Ten Tall Oaktrees' by Richard Edwards. Here, the traditional counting down style, from ten trees to no trees is used skilfully to highlight environmental issues and to show how many people want to use the oak trees, from King Henry's warships to the modern developer, as this edited version shows:

> Ten tall oaktrees
> Standing in a line,
> 'Warships,' cried King Henry,
> Then there were nine.
>
> Seven tall oaktrees,
> Branches, leaves and sticks,
> 'Firewood,' smiled the merchant,
> Then there were six.
>
> Three tall oaktrees
> Groaning as trees do,
> 'Unsafe,' claimed the council,
> Then there were two.

This delightful picture book ends with all the trees felled, but with a small ray of hope, depicted in the wordless images of the child planting and watering his acorn, and proudly watching it grow. It invites discussion about its issues, but also about the form in which it is written, a counting down poem, and the portrayal of the people who take away the trees, through their one word speeches and the reporting verbs used to describe their manner of speech:

> 'Floorboards,' beamed the builder
> 'Barrels,' boomed the brewery
> 'Progress,' snarled the by-pass
> 'Nuisance,' grumped the farmer.

Deleting the rhymes in a short poem can provide a focus for talking about which words rhyme and why: it is a version of cloze procedure but is not used in any way to assess children's reading. Discussion will make explicit their understanding of and response to the structure of the poem. This example is by Roger McGough and uses similes in an overt way. The words which could be deleted are in brackets:

The Writer Of This Poem

> The writer of this poem
> is taller than a tree
> As keen as the North wind
> As handsome as can be
>
> As bold as (a boxing glove)
> As sharp as (a nib)
> As strong as (scaffolding)
> As tricky as (a fib)
>
> As smooth as (a lolly-ice)
> As quick as (a lick)
> As clean as (a chemist-shop)
> As clever as (a ✓)
>
> The writer of this poem
> Never ceases to amaze
> he's one in a million billion
> (or so the poem says!)

Poetic and interesting uses of language are not, of course, confined to poetry. Many children's books use language in funny, unusual ways which can be discussed and described. In *How Tom Beat Captain Najork and his Hired Sportsmen* by Russell Hoban, Aunt Fidget Wonkham-Strong, a name to conjure with, hires Captain Najork to sort out her nephew, Tom. 'She is so fearsome that where she walked the flowers drooped, and when she sang the trees shivered,' a personification that captures perfectly the iron in her character.

The game to which Captain Najork challenges Tom is an amalgam of all sorts of messy children's fun, but played with a reverence accorded normally to real sport, and Hoban invents words to describe the various aspects of the game: *sneeding, grapples, wombled, snetch, tonged the bobble*. And when Captain Najork loses, but is compensated by marrying Aunt Fidget, much to Tom's relief, Tom advertises for a new aunt, and employs Aunt Bundlejoy Cosysweet.

There are rich language possibilities inherent in a book of this quality. Children can create their own game for Tom and Captain Najork to play, using invented terminology for procedures and scoring. They can place Aunt Fidget Wonkham-Strong in a new context and describe her effect on her surroundings. They can create new relatives for Tom, and name them accordingly.

In *The Little Boat* by Kathy Henderson, illustrated by Patrick Benson, the text is written as a narrative in free verse. It tells of a polystyrene boat's voyage across an ocean and simile and metaphor are used to great effect: boats in the distance on the horizon are described as 'like a toy hanging in the air at the rim of the world'; the boat, on being spat out by a fish, emerges 'like the flight of an arrow towards the light' as it 'burst through the silver skin of the sea'. The sea is descibed as 'heavy sliding gliding breathing water'. Using this model, children could write additional adventures for the little boat, such as meeting an octopus or negotiating debris, and could draw new illustrations.

William Mayne's *Lady Muck* uses stunningly innovative language forms to tell the tale of two pigs, Boark and Soark, who snuffle for truffles and try to better themselves by selling rather than eating them, though their instincts are too difficult to quell. 'Go snuffly and diggy for fat sweet rooties. That will happy me Boarky dear, from grunt to squeal' urges Soark. Boark scents 'the whifflom of the greatest pigly tasties' and they anticipate 'little snack and dinner, little snap and supper'. Children can look at how Mayne has achieved this effect: often it is through appending y to the word giving the effect of a diminutive and a child-like language, such as 'I keepy going', 'No wasty', 'too hotty'. They could write more dialogue in this style and further adventures for the pigs.

In *Dr Xargle's Book of Earthhounds*, by Jeanne Willis, the illustrations and the written text combine in a complex and fascinating way to present dogs as they might be described by an alien teacher. The whole book is a mini-lecture covering all the necessary facts about dogs which an alien visitor might need to know. In fact, the illustrations both subvert the written text and collude with the (human) reader, appealing to their sense of the way things really are: 'On the floor the Earthling has placed many newspapers for the Houndlet to read'.

Metaphor is used in interesting and extended ways. Language is metaphorical when words or phrases are used in place of other words or phrases, when the substitutions are not synonymous and where the effect is to carry over (the word metaphor comes from the Greek *metaphora* meaning to transfer) a descriptive term to an object to which it is not literally applicable. This creates an implied comparison, so that slippers become *nocturnal footwear*, a ball a *bouncing sphere*, dog biscuits are *skeleton biscuits* and a tongue a *pink flannel*. Metaphor is different from simile (Latin *similis*: like) because where the relationship is implied in metaphor, in simile it is explicitly drawn. However, it is important to note that not every expression containing the word like means it is a simile. To say that a man looks like your uncle Fred is simply a statement of similarity. To say a man is like a raging bull would be a simile.

This series includes Earthlets and Earth tiggers as well as Earth hounds, and would be an excellent stimulus for the children to write their own version. Earth teachers might be a telling challenge!

WRITERS AND READERS

There is a further, important aspect of knowledge about language which can be developed through literature, and this relates to the process of reading. Moving away from a focus on the language of the text itself takes us into a consideration of how readers read and how writers construct their readers, by assuming certain things about their responses. It means that we need to pay attention to the values implicit in what is read and to consider whether we share these values or wish to read against them. Children need to come to understand that writers have intentions, that writing does not just appear in the world, but has been created, or made, by someone, possibly a number of people. They need to come to understand that writing carries values, both implicitly and explicity or overtly, and that these values can be recovered and discussed.

Non-fiction writing is often more rhetorical in this sense because the writer and his or her intentions are often more visible than in fiction writing, but there are ways in which children's fiction provides opportunities for talking about why we read things the way we do and how readers are active makers, not passive receivers, when they read. This might be described as the beginnings of critical literacy.

For example, from a diachronic point of view, writers have constructed child readers differently. A comparison of the opening pages of Rose Impey's *Who's a Clever Girl Then?* with Enid Blyton's *Five Go to Camp* demonstrates this very well:

If you think this is the kind of story where five children, armed only with a bucket and spade, catch a dangerous band of smugglers, you'd be wrong. And if you think this is the kind of story where a poor, helpless little girl is captured by a terrible gang of cut-throat pirates . . . you'd still be wrong.

'Two jolly fine tents, four groundsheets, four sleeping bags – I say, what about Timmy? Isn't he going to have a sleeping bag too?' said Dick with a grin.
'It's absolutely wizard, being allowed to go on a camping holiday all by ourselves,' said Dick. 'I never thought our parents would allow it, after the terrific adventure we had last summer, when we went off in caravans.'

A comparison of the two books invites discussion about styles of spoken language, particularly in relation to naturalism in speech and change over time in the popularity of certain expressions and forms. It also suggests a rather different relationship between writer and reader, in that Impey uses an interactive narrator who speaks directly to the reader and who makes **inter-textual** references, thereby implying a knowledgeable reader who understands the references. Why are there these differences? Do the children know of other writers who adopt a similar interactive style, or who collude with their readers in a knowing way, as Dahl so successfully does? Would children in 1948 have different expectations of writers of children's books? Why might this be the case? What books were available then?

Developing critical literacy involves developing an awareness of our own position as a reader, how we read and what the options are for our interpretations of what we read. It means that children come to understand that writing is made, constructed by a writer or writers and that readers can choose to read with the text, or against it. By this, I mean that children can consider the intentions of the writer and who the implied or intended reader is, by asking questions like 'am I the kind of person this was written for?' Through activities and discussions, children will become active rather than passive readers, able to understand that language carries values and that the reader can question and challenge those values if they wish.

Chapter 4
Children's own language

Looking at the way they use language and their own experiences of language can be a very interesting and valuable investigative project for children. It focuses attention on their knowledge about how language is related to personal identity and how it establishes and maintains relationships. It creates opportunities for children to talk about the processes of reading, writing, speaking and listening; to think about how their abilities in these three language modes were acquired and developed; and to reflect on their competence in these areas now. This involves developing an understanding of **idiolect** – the characteristic style of speech of an individual and includes the personal and idiosyncratic features of their language, such as the way they pronounce words, the particular expressions they use, the mannerisms they have in speaking. The word comes from the Greek *idio* meaning private and *lect*, as in dialect, meaning speech. It is a useful linguistic term because it recognises that no two people ever speak exactly the same. They may have the same dialect, accent, they may even come from the same family, but the way they use language will have features which make it unique to them.

Investigating their own language also means that children can look at the influence of the language of school. Schools are institutions, just as hospitals or supermarkets are, and therefore have their own characteristic ways of using language which identify them as schools. The language environment of the school is very important to children, contributing to their own use of language, and there is an expectation that they will learn to fit into the linguistic culture of the school. It is therefore essential for children to have an understanding of the nature of this linguistic environment and how it affects their own language.

The outcome of the language activities described in this section is a personal language profile, in which a portfolio of activities about the child's own language is assembled. In addition, displays for the classroom are suggested so that children can share what they have found out about their language and come to understand what each member of the class has in common, or what is different about their language experiences, and why.

ACTIVITIES ABOUT EARLY LANGUAGE DEVELOPMENT

Ask the children to question family members about the first words the children used. Are there any family memories and stories about their first utterances, particularly in terms of what were seen as mistakes that the children made? It would be useful to discuss the kinds of questions the children might ask and to write these down, for example:

1. What were my first sounds and words?
2. What language was I using? Was it English or a different language?
3. Which members of my family also spoke this language?
4. Where did I say these words?
5. What do you think I meant when I said them?
6. Did I use any funny or unusual words when I was learning to talk?

My own examples of this include the mispronunciation of the word *onion* as *onionion* which has become a private word used by family members. The children can provide photographs for display with accompanying statements about their first words and expressions, or the photos can be stuck onto a sheet of paper and put in their files. It may be necessary to relate this task to babies and young children known to the children in the class, because the children may find it hard to gather evidence about themselves. What can very young children say? It might be possible to record a young child's talk to listen to in the classroom, particularly where it shows evidence of trying out their developing understanding of words. Children can investigate the language uses of their younger siblings using similar questions to those above, but extending them to find out what the young children can actually do with language and bringing in examples.

It would be interesting to talk with the children about how they think children learn to talk. Is it through copying an adult? If so, how is it that children can produce words which they have not heard? Does babbling count as speaking? Select some of the expressions the children have come up with for discussion: are mistakes really mistakes? What about the following:

> *Child:* Can I have some wibena?
> *Mother:* What's that? Wibena? (imitating child's pronunciation)
> *Child:* No! Not wibena! Wibena! (repeating and emphasising the pronunciation)
>
> biscetti (spaghetti); roodbarb (rhubarb); I goed; I wented; feets; mouses; three mens.

Ask the children to work out what young children are doing when they *overextend* their grammatical knowledge in this way.

Ask the children to bring in any examples of early writing they can find, either things they wrote, or things written by young children they have access to. The children will need to consider what counts as writing. Does it have to be recognisable? Encourage them to bring in anything they think is writing so that you can discuss with them the purpose of early mark-making and the emergence of written forms. Did anyone help them to do this writing? Their own writing can go in their files.

Discuss how they learned to write at school. What do they remember of how this was done? Do the children remember being read to as young children? Why do adults read to children? Make a list of their favourite stories and poems from then and compare them across the class.

Discuss the children's memories of actually learning to read. What do they remember of this process and who taught them? Do they recall any of the books they used to learn to read? It may be possible to show the children a selection of reading scheme materials for beginning readers to jog their memories and so that they can discuss what they felt about the books they had to read.

ACTIVITIES ABOUT MY LANGUAGE NOW

Children are very interested in the meaning of their own names. The Anglo-Saxons had only one name, like Ethelburga; but later, following the Viking invasions, the tradition of passing on a name through a family became established. Investigate the meanings of the children's first and second names by using a dictionary containing the **etymology** of names, or *The Guinness Book of Names.* Look up the meaning and something of the history of the meaning. Some names may come from Norman French, or refer to occupations or characteristics, or refer to a place or geographical feature of a place, such as Brooks or Marsh. Some children may have religious names or special naming traditions in their family's culture. A display can be made using photographs the children bring in of themselves captioned by their name and its meaning. This data could be compared with children's parents' names, particularly in relation to the popularity of some first names.

Make a writing and reading profile for a day. Ask the children to monitor and record their own reading and writing across a day. Two examples of how to record this are given in Figures 4.1, 4.2.

These examples can be used for reading or for writing. The clock face can be made into a large template and each child's completed day can be compared and displayed. The children will need to be reminded that we read from all sorts of sources during a day and it may be necessary to put some restriction on what they record: for example, should reading images be excluded? Some examples of the reading material can be collected and displayed. This is particularly interesting in relation to ephemera, odd bits of texts that children encounter everyday, like sweet wrappers and bus tickets.

Discuss what the children are reading now. Make a list of favourite authors, illustrators and poets. Do they have books at home that they read again and again? Why do they do this? The children can make an annotated list of the books they have read in the last term or half term for their files.

READING/WRITING PROFILE 1

NAME _____ DATE _____

7AM ————————————→ 7PM

WHAT I READ/WROTE   Cornflake packet

WHERE I READ/WROTE IT   Breakfast

WHY I READ/WROTE IT   Finding out about
                             a game to send
                             for

Figure 4.1 Reading/Writing profile: 1

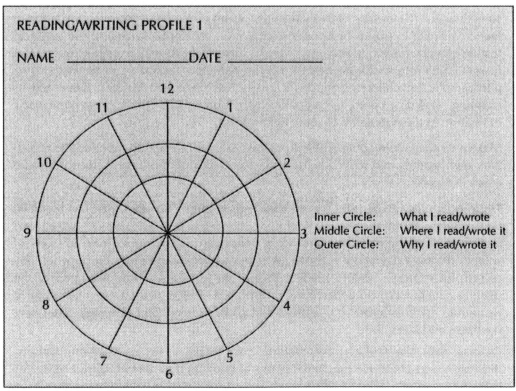

Figure 4.2 Reading/Writing profile: 2

Discuss how the children read now. Are there any favourite places where they prefer to read? Favourite places to read makes a good topic for discussion. Are some books more difficult to read than others? What makes reading difficult or easy? Make an advice sheet for display in the classroom about what to do if you don't know the meaning of a word: for example

- guess;
- use the context (words around it) to work it out;
- look it up in a dictionary;
- ask someone.

Include in the profile an example of a piece of writing which the children enjoyed creating with a commentary about why they chose this piece and why they enjoyed writing it. A sample of handwriting could also go into the profile. It would be particularly interesting to look at how each child's handwriting has changed over a period of time in aspects such as cursive handwriting, changes in the shapes of letters, idiosyncrasies in the writing, size and spacing. A whole-class activity would be to see if children could be identified from their handwriting. Signatures are closer marks of identity: how have these changed? Why are signatures so important and where are they used? Make a list of occasions when a signature is needed.

Arrange for each child to read an extract from a favourite writer or book onto tape for inclusion in their language profile. This could be accompanied by a short piece of writing about why they chose this piece and what they had to consider in reading it aloud.

ACTIVITIES ABOUT SPOKEN LANGUAGE

Discuss with the children the influences on their spoken language. This could be presented as a world map, with places marked to show where family members were born or have lived. The children could discuss the ways in which their language is influenced by their and their family's origins.

Alternatively, the children could draw or provide a family photograph and write a short language profile for each member, including things like what kind of work they do and how this influences the way they speak. The purpose of this activity is to consider what the influences are on the way we speak: these include regional origins, influence of work, friends, circles such as membership of a church, all of which contribute to the way individuals speak.

For this activity, it will be necessary to talk about the differences between *accents*, *dialects* and *languages*:

- *accent:* the features of pronunciation of a geographical region or social group;
- *dialect:* the grammar and vocabulary of a geographical region or social group;
- *language:* this is a tricky one because what makes something a language, rather than a dialect, is rather complex. It is a political as much as a linguistic question.

However, for the purposes of this activity it may be enough to look at where the children's families have come from and to name the language spoken there, if this is known, or to ask the children to find out from home.

Discuss with the children the influences on their language as they have grown up, such as the move from home to school, television, music, older children, going to church, playing out and so on. Then make a language diagram to show these influences visually. For example, this could be done as a timeline from birth to the present. This would start at birth and then indicate ages at which new language experiences happened. For example:

- saying first words;
- learning to read;
- joining the cubs/brownies;
- starting school;
- moving house;
- going on a holiday abroad.

For each of these, the children could provide examples of the new words they started to use. Another visual way of presenting this information is as a tree, with branches, or fruits on the tree, representing these significant stages. Alternatively, the children could suggest a way of representing this information.

Compile a list of words the children know from languages other than English, with their translations. Individual versions of this could go in the profile.

Are there expressions and words which the children use to each other which an outsider might not understand? Where do these come from and how do the children think they get started? Do these sayings last long? Make a list of these with their meanings and then display them as speech bubbles. These expressions and items of vocabulary can be explained through the creation of mini-dictionaries. Dictionary entries have different formats, and it will be necessary to agree a basic structure for the entries they will create: for example, the part of speech might be indicated, with an explanation of its meaning and when it is used and an example of the expression as used. For example:

cool: adjective. Usually used in a casual way. Means really good.
'That film was cool. I want to see it again on video'.

Do the children use any catchphrases or favourite expressions with their friends? How did these arise? Can the influence of television be detected, particularly in relation to game shows and children's television presenters?

Children need to understand that there are many accents of English and that these are often the cause of prejudice and discrimination. The school environment will provide some accents for discussion but the best place to find the widest selection is on the television, and particularly soaps. Make a list of people known to the children from television and the accents they have. Photographs of these people can be cut from TV magazines for a wall display. It is often the case that children think they do not have an accent, that only exaggerated or more obvious accents count as accents and that certain accents carry certain, usually derogatory associations. To what extent are they able to use more than one accent? Have they ever felt that people have disliked the way they speak or been aware of negative attitudes to their accent? How and when do they change their accent? Do they ever find themselves using the accent of the person they are speaking with? This will undoubtedly lead into a discussion of what is meant by *posh*, because the children will talk about how we change the way we speak to impress. Following discussion about this, the children can write something about their own accent, or record themselves speaking for their profile.

What songs and rhymes do the children know? Songs and rhymes we learn as children form part of our inter-textual knowledge and are passed through the generations. Ask the children to talk about songs and rhymes:

- used in games like skipping games or counting out games;
- that accompany activities like bathing the baby or going on car rides;
- that are pop songs whose lyrics they know;
- that they have learned at school, such as traditional or religious songs like Christmas carols.

Each child should select a small number of these and write out the words as they know them, then underneath answer the questions:

> *Where and when did I learn this? Who taught it to me? What is it used for? When did I last say or sing it?*

Children might ask themselves, 'Do I speak differently to different people?' Children are very much aware of the way we adjust our language so that it is appropriate to the context. Through role play, give the children a scenario which must be explained to a number of different audiences. For example: 1. Explain the rules of a game to a younger child and to an adult. What adjustments must be made? 2. Relate the events of the previous evening to a friend, your mother, a teacher, a police-officer. The children's reflections on this role-play exercise will reveal conscious and unconscious changes in what they say and how they say it and it will be important to discuss these shifts with them.

ACTIVITIES ABOUT LANGUAGE IN SCHOOL AND THE LOCALITY

The following activities are designed to enable the children to collect examples of how language is used in and around school and to reflect on the forms of language they find.

How do people speak in school? Make a list of different places in school and ask the children to suggest language they might see and hear in those places. For example:

Place	Language we see	Language we hear
kitchens	rota	are those peas ready yet?

Other places might include

the head teacher's office	the school office/secretary's office
cloakrooms	playground
staffroom	medical room
school entrance	

Take a language walk round the school. Record examples of signs and then ask the children to classify them. Possible categories are:

- *warnings* (Which could be more implied than overt, such as No Smoking);
- *instructions* (Will visitors please report to the school office/Visitors must report to the school office. What is the difference here?);
- *directions*;
- *information* (the librarian will be here each lunchtime);
- *labels* (Toilets/Medical Room).

The children could devise their own categories for the signs they gather.

In the area around the school there will be street and house names which can be investigated. House names are often unusual and idiosyncratic. If speculation about their origins is unsatisfactory, the children could write to their occupants to ask for explanations. Bartlett and Fogg (1992) carried out this activity with a Year 6 class and the children had some interesting responses to their requests:

> Our house name Jeanteca is derived from the first two letters of all of our names who live in the house. JE-Jessie, our dog, who was with us when we moved here; AN-Angie; TE-Terry; CA-Casey. I hope this helps you with your project. (p. 48)

Street names also hold etymological delights. The local library will be able to offer help in tracing the history of the names of local streets, though the children may be able to guess some origins. Local geographical features such as rivers and streams often crop up in street names, as do references to what used to be done there in the past: Mill Place, Farm Road. Street names can be taken from local maps and their names grouped: suggested groupings would include trees, county, city and town names, names associated with royalty, battles.

Shop signs often use language in interesting ways. The children could photograph a selection of unusual ones and explain why they have selected them and what interesting features the shop names have. They will find puns (Past Times), references to the goods sold by the shop (Forget-me-Not for a florist), straightforward descriptions of the business carried out (Post Office), people's names (Johnson's Shoes), alliteration (Bridal Beauty) and so on. If the locality of the school does not include a shopping centre, this information can be taken from the Yellow pages or Thomson's Local Directory. The children could guess the business from the name, or create names for shops.

Other good sources of language in the environment are road signs and general street furniture. These provide useful material for discussing the purpose of language, how it is used to make things happen or prevent them happening, to advise (Road Ahead Closed), to warn, to celebrate (This bench is dedicated to the memory of), to inform. The children can also collect examples of signs which achieve their effect without using language, like some road signs. Advertising billboards are obvious uses of language, and rubbish bins which contain any number of items with language on them (though I don't recommend that the children delve into them unsupervised!) On a recent language walk with a Year 6 group, they insisted on including the words on printed T-shirts worn by shoppers in their language list, as well as grafitti and other language which passes through the environment, such as on the sides of buses and vans. We also gathered ambiguous signs: 'Private green residents only' and my own contribution was this unintended play on words seen on the way to the school: 'Free range eggs next lay-by'.

It is important that the children discuss why the written language is there, who wrote it and with what intention.

Example of language: Sale of oriental rugs and carpets: Town Hall, Sunday 10–4. *Where I saw it:* stuck on a few lampposts; *Who I think wrote it:* someone like Del Boy or someone with no shop; *Why it was there:* to get rid of them and make money.

This will develop their understanding of the purpose of texts, because they need to understand that texts are written by people with intentions, and that they are written to achieve particular effects. They could speculate whether the examples they have collected have been produced by one or by more than one person, for example, the local council or the baker. How do signs get written?

This activity can be extended to include spoken language in the environment, such as school crossing wardens, market stall-holders, rubbish collectors, parents monitoring young children, buskers. A collage of people, activities and the spoken and written language around them would be an excellent summary of the language walk.

The children will have collected examples of language from:

- *places* where people use spoken and written language in the school;
- *different people* who use particular forms of language in their roles in the school;
- *written language* which surrounds the school.

In addition to these, and very important in the whole picture, are the languages spoken by the population of the school which contribute to its language culture. The children might conduct a survey throughout the school of languages children can read, write, speak or understand. Within the class, the question of when and with whom the languages are spoken would provide a good discussion topic and can be related to notions of language and identity.

The education system in general and schools in particular have their own language, the language of school subjects and learning. Many terms from curriculum subjects have counterparts outside and can in fact be the cause of misunderstanding for the learner. The children can provide both school and out-of-school meanings for words such as:

volume	mass
table	sentence
cell	contents
register	ruler
energy	subject

I once visited a student teacher who had asked the children to copy the table into their books, referring to a table of experimental results for seed germination which he had drawn on the board. Quite a number of the children were actually drawing the teacher's writing table in their books. He had not explained the terminology and they had used their word knowledge in good faith!

There are also some words which are more specific to the school context and which tend to be used only in that context. The children can suggest examples of these, such as SATs, dinner money, assembly.

All the activities suggested in this section are to enable the children to reflect on the language around them and the language they use, so that they can begin to see how their lives are permeated with language and that the way they experience the world is mediated by language. Reflection on their language experiences needs to be planned. It can take the form of:

- Regular conferences with children about their reading and writing.
- The setting up of language partners in the classroom, where the children act as critical readers for each other's work and can speak or write their responses. The responses to the writing can become a dialogue between teacher and child and can be influential in helping the children to shape their writing to the needs of an audience.
- A learning log or diary in which the children regularly write about their views of their own learning about language and how to use it. This could take the form of statements about how they feel about the quality of their work, preferred ways of writing and reading, strategies they use to cope with challenging reading, range of writing activities over a fortnight etc.
- The establishment of ground rules for talk in the classroom, where the children discuss and agree a wording for the way talk should be conducted in the classroom. Children can act as detectives checking on whether any of the agreed rules are being broken.
- Discussion about what makes a good listener and how to be a helpful response partner.

Suggestions about listening could be included in the ground rules for talk.

Chapter 5

Working with words

This section suggests activities for looking more closely at words, their forms and meanings and how they are used. The intention is to put language under a microscope, so that children can see how flexible and variable it can be, and can play around with words. The Kingman Report (DES 1988) argued that 'In what might be called the carpentry of life, language should be the sharpest instrument' (p. 7).

Engaging children in activities which require close attention to language may contribute to their interest in and ability to use language, but this should not necessarily be seen as a justification for studying language: language is interesting in its own right and looking at language should be an everyday part of the work of the classroom. It could be argued that there is a danger in the activities because they are decontextualised, but they are a far cry from the grammar exercises referred to earlier. They allow for play with language, for learning about unusual and interesting aspects of language. Their focus is language as it is used and they build on the working knowledge of language which children have. The activities can be used as occasional, one-off activities, or a selection of them could be made into a mini-language project. The suggestions here are examples and can be adapted to suit the needs of a particular class.

ACTIVITIES WITH WORDS

The Alphabet

To reinforce alphabetical order, write an A to Z for a hobby, or a game. The entries could be short or extended so that the text becomes more of an information text. Team games to find words in the dictionary will test knowledge of alphabetical order beyond the first letter, as will locating information in the *Yellow Pages* or similar sources of information.

Dictionaries

Look at how different dictionaries organise their entries. Compare entries for one word. Ask the children to list what they think the differences are. Discuss what they think the abbreviations mean, such as *adj. v.* (they will need to know some of the parts of speech for this). Choose some common, everyday words, for example *put* or *see* and look them up and compare them with some uncommon words. Why are common words more likely to have much longer entries than uncommon words?

Where do the compilers get their definitions from? The children will see that some are based on speech and some on literary references. Which do they think is the more valid? Create definitions for some common words or words which the children use and compare them with dictionary entries. Subversive entries can be also be written, giving incorrect definitions, for example a Martian's dictionary written with only superficial knowledge of the English language.

Look at a supplement to a dictionary and explain that these are words that had to be added when the dictionary was reprinted (the difference between printing and re-printing may need to be explained here). Which words are new and which are additions to or extensions of original meanings? Are there any surprising inclusions? Try to explain why these words had to be in the supplement.

Words from other languages

Understanding that language is dynamic and must grow and change to meet the needs of its speakers is an important aspect of knowledge about language. Children need to understand that changes in language are inevitable and that English as spoken now is the result of borrowings from and historical relationships with other languages. For example, the children are probably unaware of the number of words we use in English which have come from Greek and Latin. The relationship of English to these two languages will need to be briefly explained, as will the fact that Latin is no longer spoken.

Consider some Latin and Greek prefixes, such as the following, and ask the children to find as many words as they can which use them:

Greek: geo: earth; micro: small; bio: life; auto: self; tele: far.
Latin: centi: a hundred; im: not; semi: half; super: above or outstanding.

The following common English words come from other languages. Using an etymological dictionary, the children can find out where the words originated. Ask the children to speculate about why these words were brought from other languages (for example, trade, colonisation, travel, emigration).

yoghurt	kangaroo
tobacco	jungle
chop suey	sugar
banquet	mosquito
maize	shampoo
menu	bungalow
robot	anorak
coffee	

Place names reveal something of the history of invasion and settlement of the British Isles. The children can find local placenames from a map of the area which reveal some of their history. For example, they can look for:

Celtic: combe: valley; *lan:* church.
Anglo-Saxon: ham: village; *wick:* dairy farm; *ton:* enclosure.
Roman: castle/caster/cester/cister: walled town; *port:* sea landing.
Scandinavian: thorpe: farm; *by:* village.

The children can suggest names for new towns based on these meanings.

The meanings of words

Playing games like 'Call my Bluff' will encourage the children to think about the structures of words and their etymology. This game may not be familiar to the children, but it is worth setting up a simplified version of the television programme. In teams, the children either choose, or are given, unusual words from the dictionary. They then create two spoof definitions for them and look up the real one. The task is for an opposing team to listen to the three definitions and to guess which is the correct one. The spoof definitions need to be plausible, to have an air of validity about them, which can be a challenge to write, and the definitions need to match the word in terms of the part of speech. I would recommmend that the words selected should be nouns or verbs to begin with. The listening team should justify why they have chosen a particular definition, rather than just opting for one and should have time to discuss the words.

A slightly simpler version of this is for the teacher to give the teams three written definitions for words. This would be a good preparation for moving on to the more challenging version.

Metaphor and idiom

Metaphor is not simply a poetic device or something that exists solely in poetry. Lakoff and Johnson (1980) describe the essence of metaphor as 'understanding and experiencing one kind of thing in terms of another'. The English language is permeated with metaphor: it is very difficult not to use metaphor in our everyday speech. We speak of arguments in terms of war (attack someone's position, win and lose, defend a position); we speak of time in terms of money (waste it, spend it, save it); love as madness (insane, mad about the girl, wild about Harry). To understand how intrinsic these metaphors are to our way of thinking and experiencing, Lakoff and Johnson suggest trying to conceive of something in quite different terms from the way it is actually conceived: for example, an argument as a dance. The whole conceptual framework shifts and the cultural specificity of these metaphors is made more apparent.

Idioms are expressions whose meaning as a whole is greater than the meaning of any individual part of the expression. The meaning of an idiom like 'I spilled the beans', cannot be recovered from the actual words. Either brainstorm with the children a list of idioms they know and discuss their meaning, or provide the children with a list for discussion. How would they explain the meaning of these? For example:

- to kick the bucket; to save someone's bacon; to turn over a new leaf; to take something with a pinch of salt.

It is important for children to talk about the metaphorical nature of language, how language is rarely literal. One starting point is to investigate common expressions: what do some of the following mean? It is an interesting task to consider their literal meanings and to illustrate them accordingly:

- hold your horses; keep your hair on; he's two sandwiches short of a picnic (and other similar versions); stop beating about the bush; I'm in at the deep end; it was touch and go; she twisted my arm; he flipped his lid; look before you leap; a stitch in time saves nine.

Synonyms, antonyms, homonyms, homophones and homographs

These words are distinctive in different ways. **Synonyms** are loosely defined as words with the same meaning, which could substitute for each other. In practice, words very rarely denote exactly the same thing: there are nuances of difference which are necessary, otherwise the word would drop out of use. Synonymy allows shades of meaning. Collecting synonyms will provoke useful discussion about these nuances. For example, ask the children to find synonyms for *hot* or *big*. What are the differences between these words and in what context might they be appropriate?

sweating, boiling, baking, roasting, sweltering.

massive, huge, large, gigantic, mega, immense, ginormous.

Similar activities to generate discussion about word meanings are possible with antonyms.

Antonyms are words which are opposite in meaning, but again this is a loose definition. Linguists distinguish between *gradable* and *ungradable* antonyms, because some opposites are more absolute than others: for example, dead and alive, male and female are ungradable but old and young, big and small are gradable. There are also *relational* antonyms which express reciprocity, such as lend and borrow, buy and sell.

Homonyms are words which are spelled and pronounced the same way, but which have different meanings. Ask the children to find as many meanings as they can for the following words: they should try this without using a dictionary to begin with, then see how many more versions they can find by looking them up. They should also identify the part of speech.

bar	litter
set	bank
mint	charge
catch	screen

Homophones are words which sound the same but are different in meaning and spelling. These often cause difficulties in writing when the writer is over-dependent on phonetic spelling. The children can keep a list of these for reference as they meet them. Ask them to use these words to show their different meanings:

freeze/frieze	tail/tale
stair/stare	deer/dear
weather/whether	peace/piece
sail/sale	not/knot
horse/hoarse	fare/fair

Homographs are words which have the same spelling but different pronunciation and meaning:

Lead/lead	produce/produce	desert/desert	does/does	sewer/sewer
refuse/refuse	object/object	row/row		

Suffixes and prefixes

These are both **affixes** and affixation is an aspect of morphology, the forming of words. Prefixes change the nature of the word, for example, rendering it negative or oppositional. Ask the children to form words from these prefixes:

mis: mistake misread misunderstand
un: unhappy uncomfortable unexciting
dis: dishonest dislike disapprove

Note that *un* creates reverses as well as negatives, which may need to be pointed out: *unroll, undo, unpick.*

The number of suffixes in English is so great that it is impossible to discuss them all here. In essence, suffixes change the grammatical class of words. The children can look at some common suffixes, finding words which end in

-ation	-ment
-ly	-less

Alternatively this can be done the other way round: find the word that has been changed to make:

preservation	relation
statement	payment
gratefully	firmly
piglet	gardener
hopeless	

Tongue-twisters and riddles

Children can have great fun writing tongue-twisters for each other. These are usually elaborate examples of alliteration and closely related consonants, for example *s/sh* distinctions as in *she sells sea shells on the sea shore.*

Formulaic riddles (for example, *My first is in flower but not in fire*) develop children's sense of word patterns and shapes because a word is built up from letter clues and only certain letter strings are possible. They also help to reinforce word meanings because the final line is a description of the target word: *My whole guides the ships home safely from sea.*

Writing in code

Creating and breaking codes reinforces spelling. Codes can be alphabetical, substituting letters for letters; they can use symbols for letters or can use pictures to represent words. A distinction can be drawn between:

- *rebus:* a combination of pictures and letters to represent the syllables of the word, but without any direct relevance to the word itself;
- *pictogram:* the referent is represented as a picture, so a picture of the sun represents the sun;
- *ideogram:* pictures are used to express ideas, not just objects.

Familiarise the children with the concept of a symbol by compiling a list of symbols with which they are familiar, such as £, &, %, =, +, $, x. Then introduce:

- road sign symbols;
- trademark symbols like McDonald's;
- stylised symbols for men and women.

Gesture and mime

Compile a list of everyday gestures, avoiding the most obviously problematic ones if possible! What do they signify? For example, waving, nodding and shaking the head, a gesture to sit down, pointing etc. Discuss why we use these and how difficult it is to communicate without them: play a question and answer reversal game where a nod means no and a shake of the head means yes. Where do we see particular gestures used? In groups, the children could look at one situation or place and list the gestures we might expect to see there, such as transport (moving planes, a guard at a station), in sports (sending off, full-time, out in cricket).

An interesting way of focusing on gesture is to look at a video without the sound. The chidren then have to look closely at gesture and what it might signify, since the spoken language is not there. Then turn up the sound and compare. As an extension to this, the children can write down what they think is being said in these contexts, deducing this from the facial expression and gesture. I find *Today in Parliament* a very useful resource for this, or an interview, guest/host programme. The notion of gesture can be extended to include general body language. Through improvisation, look at how interest or boredom is conveyed. Miming everyday activities will focus attention on this: make a cup of tea in a temper, do the shopping in a way which indicates sadness.

Language changing

Compare a current children's television programme with one from the past: some of the early *Watch with Mother* and other children's programmes from the early days of television are available on video. What differences can the children see? Smith (1992) describes a very interesting project where her class investigated these differences in relation to *Take Hart* from 1990 and *Picture Book* from 1963. They looked at very brief extracts from each programme and in terms of language found:

- changes in the use of words (jolly, super);
- changes in voice quality and accent (a high pitched RP was used in *Picture Book*);
- differences in body language (formality);
- changes in the nature of the language of explanation.

There were, of course, other differences of a non-linguistic nature, such as camera techniques and clothes. Each group was given one aspect to watch for and make notes on. A similar comparison of a published advert can reveal significant changes in the approach to selling, in the language of advertising and the implied consumer.

Reading English which is different from contemporary English can enable children to understand how language has changed. Read the children a modern version of one of The Canterbury Tales, such as *The Pardoner's Tale*, and compare it with the original text. Can the children work out what the original means? Are there any words which look similar to modern words? List those that are similar and those that are identical. It would be beneficial for them to hear the original: there are a number of recordings available.

Write a glossary for an Australian soap, such as *Neighbours*. There are many words used in these programmes which are not used frequently in this country. Watch a short extract together, list any words which might need explanations and then write the meanings. For example: *to be crook:* to be ill; *g'day:* hello; the use of the word *mate*.

Create new names for new products. Suggest appropriate names for the following and explain why this name is suitable: a new car; a new biscuit; a perfume; a hairstyle; a new style of training shoe; a potato snack; a fizzy drink.

An advert for the product can be designed.

Word games

The possibilities are endless but here are some suggestions:

- invent onomatopoeic words for everyday sounds, such as the noise the shower makes as it starts;
- make as many words as possible out of another word;
- make anagrams from a sentence;
- make crosswords in groups for other groups to complete;
- create new rhyming slang, then use the rhymes in a story;
- find as many ways as possible of spelling the O sound in *open* and the A sound in *stay*, such as: *sew, though, bow,* or *great, late, straight*.

Chapter 6

Working with texts

This section looks at activities which will enable children to understand the nature of different types of writing and their purposes. Through considering the purposes and audience for a range of different types of writing, children will be thinking about these issues in relation to their own work. They will begin to learn about the nature of writing and how meaning is made in the context of whole texts.

ACTIVITIES WITH TEXTS

A tub of texts

This activity introduces children to a range of texts in everyday use, drawing their attention to the number of different types of writing we encounter and the functions of these texts. It raises questions about where texts come from and what people do with them and it demonstrates that texts have purposes.

Fill a tub with as many different texts as possible. Some possibilities would be:

menu	school brochure	recipe
bus ticket	estate agents' details for a property	map
poem	catalogue	receipt
birthday card	printed food wrapper	seed packet with
advert	Yellow Pages	planting instructions
comic	telephone directory	letter
magazine article	instructions for playing a game	money-off voucher
newspaper article	a completed cheque	gas bill

Different groups can be given different tubs. The task is to select a text and answer these questions about it:

What is it?
Where would you find it?
What do people use it for?
Who would use it?
Where would people read it?
Who wrote it?
Why did they write it?

One or two texts could be modelled for the whole class before letting the children do this in smaller groups, writing their answers following discussion. The children should be encouraged to look at the writing in the text, at the information it conveys, rather than simply to name the text, most of which they should be familiar with or should be able to work out a purpose for.

A warm-up activity for this would be to ask the children to turn out their pockets/bags to collect as many texts as possible.

The text game

This activity is an adaptation and simplified version of the one produced in the Language in the National Curriculum (LINC) training materials. The purpose of this card game is to focus on the audience and purpose of a text. The children are given cards in three categories: audiences/readers; purposes; and forms or types of text. Turning over a card from each category, they have to write the text that would emerge from the combination they have created. So turning over friend, explain and postcard would require the children to explain something to a friend in the form of a postcard and would mean that children needed a good understanding of the kind of text they would have to write. Level 1 is easier than Level 2 because the text types are more familiar and are more easily adapted to the purpose. The audience too is more accessible. Level 2 provides four categories (writer is added), so that the children are writing more in role. The characters are rather removed from the real and the text types are more challenging.

In the first version, the children need to create a person who would be writing and a context for the writing: the story behind it. They should be encouraged to think who might be writing this. Any substitutions can be made to the cards and new categories created: for example, a content category could be added. Characters from books being read in the class could be used.

Level 1

Reader/Audience	Purpose		Form
Friend	Persuade	Describe	Letter
Parent	Explain	Instruct	Postcard
Teacher	Organise	Complain	Newspaper Article

Level 2

Audience			
The Queen	Michael Owen	Bart Simpson	
	Father Christmas	Seven Dwarves	Harry Potter

Writer			
Snow White	Cinderella	Batman	Robin Hood
Pokemon character	Prime Minister	Eastenders character	

Purpose			
Argue	Warn	Complain	Explain
Entertain			

Form			
Recipe	Rap	Letter excusing you	Invitation to a party
Police Report		from PE	

Paired groups could set a challenge for each other to create a text given an audience, a purpose and a text type.

Where is this from?

These next two activities ask the children to identify where snippets of speech and writing come from. Where might they hear the following?

> 'Two fifties please.'
> 'Only one pound fifty a kilo.'
> 'Let us pray.'
> 'Good morning everyone.'
> 'Do you want chips?'
> 'That'll be four pounds seventy.'
> 'Right, get changed everyone.'

Where might they see these written?

> 'First wash and peel the potatoes.'
> 'New to market. No forward chain. Four beds, gch, garage, parking. £175,000 ono.'
> 'Convenient apartment close to beach. View of sea from first floor balcony. Available in July and early August.'
> 'Each player takes the picture card and places it in the rack. The first player throws the dice.'
> 'This product must be assembled and operated in accordance with these instructions and used only for domestic cleaning to remove dry dust and dirt on household carpets and flooring.'
> 'Because of a tricky aspect between the sun and Pluto it would be best to keep business and pleasure completely separate this week.'
> 'Your child should bring a packed lunch and warm clothing for the trip.'
> 'Fire Door: Keep Closed at All Times.'

The children could:

- write the next sentence in the text;
- find some examples of written language to test their friends with;
- discuss why these kinds of writing exist. What is their purpose?

The fridge door

Ask the children to think about the kinds of writing there are in their homes, not just in books and magazines, but also the daily documentation which often gathers on a notice board or fridge door. Ask them to make a note of some examples from home. These might include:

money-off coupons	photos
letters from family or school	pictures drawn by the children at school
shopping lists	reminders about meetings and appointments
postcards	diaries/calendars

bills (e.g. gas bills)   birthday
recipes   dates to remember

Create a larger-than-life notice board or fridge door display for the classroom, using material written or drawn by the children.

Writing instructions for procedures

Ask the children to write the instructions for a simple, everyday activity. These are then tried out by their partners. Examples which might be possible in the classroom without too much mess would be:

- tying a tie
- wrapping a parcel
- making a sandwich
- covering a book.

The language of food labels

Look at a range of labels or panels from food products. What kind of information is there? Divide the language into *Information* and *Advertising*. Is any necessary information not included? Are there different levels of information? Which information might be legally rquired? Redesign the label for better clarity or to be more visually interesting.

Transform a genre

Take articles from the local newspaper or free newspaper and turn them into different genres, such as a play script, a narrative, a poem. The children will need help to identify the main events of the articles and need not be restricted to the characters in the real life story, but should include them.

The same articles can be rewritten for different audiences: for example, an article about pollution in the local river could be written for a fishing magazine, or an article about skip fires could be adapted for a safety leaflet for children.

Reading adverts

Look at a selection of adverts aimed at children, for example, for toys, video games, clothes. The children could bring in adverts from home. Discuss with the children why they think the adverts are aimed at them. Then use the following questions to frame the discussion:

- Who actually wrote this and who is speaking the advert? Make a list of all the people involved in the writing of the advert.
- Who is the advert speaking to? Can we tell? What kind of person is it aimed at (e.g. parents or children, environmentally aware or not, girls or boys)? Am I this kind of person?
- What is the advert trying to say? Is it trying to create a particular effect? What is this effect and how does it achieve it? Encourage the children to focus on specific features of the adverts, including language, images, music.
- What do I think of it? Do I agree with it? Do I like it or dislike it? Why?

Write some adverts which do not conform to the Advertising Standards Authorities guidelines about being legal, decent, honest and truthful. Choose a product to sell, making the most flamboyant claims. Write an advert guaranteed not to make the reader want to buy the product.

Funny genres

Give the children some unusual topics for writing in a range of genres. For example:
Write about eating school dinners as a restaurant review.
Write the estate agent's particulars for selling the school or your own home.
Write about a PE lesson as a news bulletin.
Write about the local area as a travel brochure.

Sequence chronological and non-chronological writing

Chronological writing means writing which is time-related, such as a narrative, an account of a visit, a procedure. Non-chronological writing does not have this organising feature, as shown, for example, in an argument about the new bypass, or a piece of writing about pets. The two categories are not exclusive and there are many examples where they coexist in one text quite readily. Nevertheless, it is useful for children to understand the differences and a sequencing activity will require some careful thought about coherence and the organisation of information and ideas in both kinds of writing. Give the children examples of both, cut up into sentences or, slightly easier, sections, marking each section with a letter or a number. Ask the children to reconstruct the original and to discuss and compare the order they choose.

Generate criteria for writing particular genres

Here the children demonstrate their understanding of particular genres through writing the 'rules' for them. They could, for example, write in role as a newspaper editor explaining how to write a TV review or football report, or write an advice sheet for new writers on how to write a good short story for a magazine. This could be structured as a Dos and Don'ts list. In pairs, they could then use each other's guidelines and create the text.

Write the text for a catalogue

Photocopy a page from a catalogue such as the Argos catalogue or one of the many such catalogues which come through the door as junk mail. Delete the descriptive text about the items portrayed and ask the children to write their own text to describe them. A similar approach can be taken to the photographs from holiday brochures, or of houses from estate agents' material. The text can be annotated to indicate which parts the children think are true and which not true.

Scrambled texts 1

Take random sentences from newspaper articles about similar topics. Discuss why this doesn't make sense to the reader and how we expect thematic coherence when we read, that is, that we do not expect things to leap around like this and do expect the writer to take an issue or idea and develop it in some way, however briefly.

Scrambled texts 2

Mix two texts together, randomly, and ask the children to work out which is which and to write each one out. For example:

- two pieces from information texts on different subjects (same genre, different topic);
- an extract from a story and an information book which are broadly about the same thing (different genre, same topic);
- an extract from a tabloid newspaper and one from a broadsheet dealing with the same news item.

Using literature to write a range of genres

The experience of reading a play or a novel can provide an excellent stimulus for writing different kinds of texts. These examples of different genres (Figure 6.1) come from a project on the teaching of *Macbeth* to Year 6 in a London school (Language in the National Curriculum Broadsheets, 1992). Here, significant moments from the play were selected for drama activities, providing a context for the writing, some of which was in role. The teacher used writing to fix the story for the children and they produced these very successful examples of writing in genres.

- **Letters – an extract of a letter written by Macbeth to Lady Macbeth after meeting the witches**

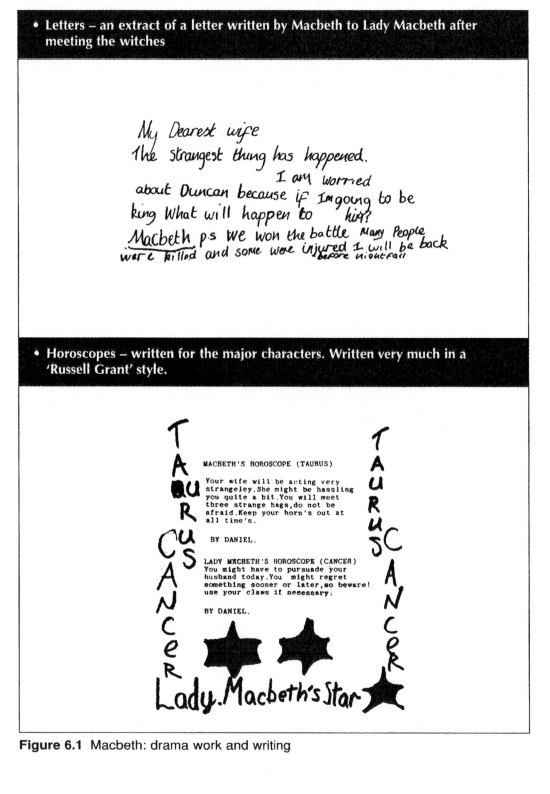

- **Horoscopes – written for the major characters. Written very much in a 'Russell Grant' style.**

Figure 6.1 Macbeth: drama work and writing

- **Diary writing** – an extract from the doctor's diary after seeing Lady Macbeth sleepwalking.

I had a very exciting night last night...
...suddenly Queen Macbeth came out of her
room. I felt embarrassed. Should I be seeing
the queen in her nightgown? I closed my
eyes. The servant told me to watch. The
queen was rubbing her hands. She was
sleepwalking. She began to talk "Will these
hands ne'er be clean?" I looked at her
hands- they were clean as a whistle. What
was she talking about? She carried on
talking. "Yet who would have thought the old
man to have had so much blood in him" I
froze solid, could our Queen possibly be a
murderer? Have all these crimes been
committed by a lady? I wanted to be at home,
I should never have come out. The gold table
seemed to turn to stone. I quickly left I
prayed no-one would find out.

- **Newspaper reports** – A newspaper report 'tabloid' style on Macbeth's strange behaviour at the banquet.

king gets
shamed by
QUEEN

king macbeth

Kung sees ghost

King macbeth aged 38
Says he saw a ghost,
The ghost of Banquo
who was mysterious
killed while on a
hunting trip.

Mr. Horthorn who
saw this out rage
said "hes gone mad"
the queen shouted at
him to try to make
him shut up. quote:
shut up you bumbling fool
(out loud) more by Sir Gibso

Figure 6.1 continued

Endnote

This book has argued that learning to use language and learning about language are essential aspects of the English curriculum. That curriculum is the continuing subject of wide-ranging debate and controversy about what English is and its purpose in the curriculum. The NLS is a very influential contribution to the debates, though it has not settled them, and there remain fundamental questions about its content and orientation. Its emphasis, largely on competence, does not exclude but does largely neglect the crucial significance of reflection on the nature and functions of language in a more extended and sustained way. Much more research is needed into the impact on primary children's literacy development of different kinds of language study, including the teaching of grammatical functions, and with a concern for reading as well as writing. Using language creatively and competently, studying critically how people use it and what it can do, should be at the heart of the English curriculum. It is this critical approach, the development in all children of a critical literacy which must be placed alongside political and public exhortations to develop children's basic skills in literacy. There is nothing basic in these skills and little point in acquiring them unless you can use them for powerful and creative purposes.

Glossary

This Glossary contains terms which teachers need to know and includes terms which children may encounter in the National Curriculum and the NLS. The explanations given are deliberately short and necessarily selective.

ABSTRACT NOUN
A category of noun which refers to abstract entities such as feelings and concepts.

ACCENT
The pronunciation characteristic of a region or a social group.

ACTIVE (AND PASSIVE) VOICE
The action of a clause can be expressed in two ways: *the birds ate the fruit* or *the fruit was eaten by the birds*.
The first of these is in the active voice and the second in the passive. The active voice is where the subject of the verb is also the agent of (the thing that carries out) the action. The passive voice is where the object of the verb (the fruit) is moved to the front of the clause and becomes, in effect, a passive subject. In passive constructions it is often impossible to identify the agent of the verb and this ambiguity can be exploited: *the money was taken from my purse.*

ADDRESSER/ADDRESSEE
In spoken and written communication, the person who sends the communication and the person to whom it is addressed.

ADJACENCY PAIRS
Formulaic or anticipated responses in conversation: where one utterance requires another in response, such as a question requiring an answer or a greeting requiring a greeting.

ADJECTIVE
A word which describes or modifies a noun.

ADVERB
A word which describes the action expressed by a verb.

AFFIX
The part of a word which is added to a root word to change its meaning or status. At the front it is a *prefix* and the end it is a *suffix*.

AGENT
The person or thing performing the verb.

ALLITERATION
Especially in poetry, the repetition of sounds at the beginnings of words for particular effect.

ALVEOLAR
Sounds produced using the teethridge (alveolus) or hard palate.

ANAPHORIC/ANAPHORA
Particularly in relation to cohesion, that is, the links between sentences, reference to something which has already been referred to: backwards reference. Typically, this will be a link between a pronoun in one sentence and a noun in a preceding sentence: *I opened **the parcel. It** contained four smaller parcels.*

ANTONYM
A word opposite in meaning to another word.

ASSONANCE
Especially in poetry, the repetition of vowel sounds for particular effect.

BILABIAL
Sounds produced by putting the lips together, as in *p* and *b*.

BLEND
In Phonics, the blending of two or more phonemes such as *st, cl, sp, cr, spl.*

CATAPHORIC/CATAPHORA (*see* ANAPHORIC)
Reference forward to something which is to come: ***This***, *it seemed, was the problem. No-one had remembered to bring the key.*

CHRONOLOGICAL/NON-CHRONOLOGICAL
The way in which the content of a written text is organised: if it is organised according to a real or imagined sequence of time, it is chronological. If time sequence is not a feature of the organisation, as in a description or a report, this is non-chronological.

CLAUSE
A unit of language, containing at least a subject and a verb, which forms part of a sentence. Independent clauses are clauses which themselves make a simple sentence. Coordinated clauses are two clauses in a sentence joined together by a conjunction. The clauses may be equally important. Main clauses make sense on their own and could be independent clauses, but they have a subordinate clause with them in the sentence. Subordinate clauses do not make sense on their own and need to attach themsleves to a main clause.

CLIPPED FORM
Where a new word-form is created by cutting off parts of the original word, as in *aeroplane* becoming *plane* or *limo* deriving from *limousine.*

COHESION
The way in which a text holds together and makes sense. This is achieved principally through grammatical relationships (the way elements are linked through the grammar) and lexical ones (through the use of related words, repetition etc.).

COLLECTIVE NOUN
A category of noun which refers to a group or collection, such as a *school* of whales.

COMMON NOUN
As distinct from proper nouns, common nouns encompass the three categories of *abstract, collective* and *concrete* nouns.

COMPARATIVE
The form of the adjective or adverb which makes a comparison, as in *big, bigger, fast, faster.* It can also be expressed using *more,* as in *more appropriate.*

COMPETENCE
A term used by Chomsky to describe a speaker's underlying knowledge of language, as distinct from a speaker's actual use of language (performance).

CONCRETE NOUN
A category of noun which refers to physical entities or phenomena.

CONJUNCTION
A word which joins clauses together, such as *and, but, so* etc.

CONTEXT OF SITUATION
A concept which recognises that meaning arises from the context in which language is used. This context encompasses non-material matters such as relationships and participants' knowledge. The context of situation may be nothing at all to do with the actual physical environment of the act of speaking or writing.

COUNT/NON-COUNT NOUNS
Count nouns are individual, countable items, such as *cars* or *oranges.* Non count nouns cannot be individually counted, as in *death* or *music.* However, in some contexts it is possible for words which are normally non-counts to be counted, as in *two teas.*

DECLARATIVES
Sentences which make a statement.

DEEP STRUCTURE
In transformational grammar, the underlying grammatical relations and structures, as distinct from the surface or apparent structure of sentences.

DEFINITE/INDEFINITE ARTICLE
The definite article is *the.* The indefinite articles are *a* and *an.*

DEICTIC REFERENCE
In cohesion, words or phrases which refer to things in the text without actually naming them: *We must go **there** and sort **this** out.*

DEMONSTRATIVES
This, that, these, those.

DIACHRONIC VARIATION
The way language changes over time. Synchronic variation refers to variation at a given point in time.

DIALECT
A regional and social variety of a language, its grammar and vocabulary.

DIALECTAL VARIATION
The way language varies because of the user's usage, such as in regional and social varieties.

DIATYPIC VARIATION
The way language varies in relation to the uses to which it is put, such as in the differing structures of written texts.

DIGRAPH
In Phonics, two letters which represent one phoneme, such as th, ch, gh.

DIPHTHONGS
Vowel sounds which begin with one sound and move towards another.

DISCOURSE ANALYSIS
The analysis and categorisation of naturally occurring spoken language.

DISJUNCT
Adverbials which sit outside the clause and enable the speaker/writer to express attitudes to the clause itself: *Regrettably, the event did not take place.*

ELISION
In speech or writing, dropping a letter or syllable, as in *don't.*

ELLIPSIS
The omission of part of a sentence, acceptable because the omitted words are implied and recoverable from the context.

ETYMOLOGY
The study of the origins of words.

EXCLAMATORY
Sentences which express with emphasis the way something is done: *He scored a goal!*

EXOPHORIC
In cohesion, the use of words to refer to something outside the text.

EXPANDED NOUN PHRASE
A group of words which acts as a noun: ***The dashing, debonair sword-swallower from the circus*** came to tea.

EXPLICIT (KNOWLEDGE)
In contrast to implicit understanding, the understanding of language in a more conscious way.

EXPOSITORY
Types of writing which are non-narrative and more factual in orientation, such as arguments or reports.

FACE
An individual's sense of self which is affected by linguistic interaction with other people.

FELICITY CONDITIONS
The external conditions necessary to enable linguistic actions to have real effects in the

world. For example, only a judge or magistrate is literally permitted to sentence a guilty person, even though anyone is permitted to say the words *I sentence you to three years*.

FIELD
The subject or content of a text.

FRICATIVES
Sounds produced by pushing air through a constriction, causing friction, as in *f* and *s*.

GRAMMATICAL WORDS
Words which have no intrinsic meaning out of context but which have a grammatical function, such as *because, it, so* etc.

GRAPHEME
In Phonics, the representation of a sound in writing.

HEADWORD
A noun which is the key word, or head, of a noun phrase: *Little hairy* **spiders** *are frightening*.

HEDGES
Ways in which speakers lessen the impact of what they are saying, to protect the addressee's sense of self or face: *Do you think there's any chance that you could take this for me?*

HOMOGRAPHS
Words with the same spelling but different pronunciation and meaning.

HOMONYMS
Words with the same spelling and pronunciation but a different meaning.

HOMOPHONES
Words with the same pronunciation but different spelling and meaning.

HYPONYM
Hyponymy describes the relationship between lexical items, that is between specific examples and general categories. Hyponyms of cutlery are knife, fork, spoon. Cutlery is known as the super-ordinate.

IDEATIONAL
A term used by Halliday to refer to the learning or thinking function of language.

IDIOLECT
The language spoken by an individual, encompassing regional and social forms, including idiosyncratic features.

IDIOM
A fixed expression where the meaning is more than the literal meaning of the actual words in the expression, such as in *to save someone's bacon*.

ILLOCUTION
The intention behind the words of a speaker.

IMPERATIVES
Sentences which are orders or instructions.

IMPLICATURE
The meaning of an utterance which is beyond the literal, semantic meaning of the words used: an implied meaning.

IMPLICIT (KNOWLEDGE)
(See EXPLICIT) Unconscious understanding about language.

INDIRECT OBJECT
The recipient of the action of the verb in a clause or sentence: *He gave the book to **her***.

INTERPERSONAL
A term used by Halliday in his functional model of language to refer to the role of language in establishing and maintaining relationships.

INTERROGATIVES
Sentences which are questions.

INTER-TEXTUAL
References or allusions within texts to other texts.

INTRANSITIVE
Verbs which do not take an object, such as *wait* or *fall*. Transitive verbs take a direct object, as in *eat* (food).

LANGUAGE
The use of sounds and written language to communicate and to think.

LANGUE
A term used by Saussure for the abstract system of language.

LEXICAL DENSITY
The ratio of lexical items to grammatical items in a sentence or clause, indicating the density of the information presented.

LEXICAL WORDS
Words which carry semantic meaning, as distinct from *grammatical words*.

LEXIS
An aspect of the study of vocabulary which describes all the words in a language.

LOAN WORD
A word from one language which is adopted and used by another language.

LOCUTION
The actual words of an utterance.

METACOGNITIVE
An awareness of, and reflection on, the processes of one's own learning and understanding.

METALANGUAGE
A language for talking about and describing language.

METAPHOR
A metaphor is an expression in which something is described as though it were something else, to suggest a closeness between the two. Metaphor is common in everyday language as well as being used in more literary contexts.

MODE
In a functional model of language, the medium of communication, such as spoken or written language, and the role played by the language – what the language does.

MORPHEMES
The small units from which words are formed.

MORPHOLOGY
The study of word structure.

MORPHO-PHONEMIC
The correspondence of sound to units of words (morphemes).

NASAL
Sounds which are formed by the resonance of air in the nasal cavities, as in *m*.

NEOLOGISM
A new word in the lexicon.

NEUTRAL VOWEL
Also called *schwa*. The most common vowel sound in English, but it does not have a corresponding alphabetic letter. It is made in the centre of the mouth when the tongue is at rest, for example in the last sound of *after*.

NOMINALISATION
The process of forming a noun from another word class, such as a verb becoming a noun, as in *to close* becoming *closure*.

NON-FINITE
Finite verbs indicate tense, number and mood, as in *I worked* (past), *they work* (number) and *he should work* (mood). Non-finite ones do not: they remain the same in the clause, regardless of tense, number and mood. There are three non-finite forms of the verb: the *-ing* form, the *-ed* participle and the infinitive, as in *I am working, I worked* and *to work*.

NOUN
A class of words which names people, things, places, concepts etc.

OBJECT
Grammatically, the direct object of a sentence relates directly to the verb and usually follows it, as in *I enjoy the **theatre***. See also INDIRECT OBJECT.

ONOMATOPOEIA
Where a word imitates the sound of the thing it represents, as in *splash* or *buzz*.

ONSET
In Phonics, the initial consonant in a syllable.

PARALINGUISTIC
Aspects of language, such as body language, which are non-verbal.

PAROLE
A term used by Saussure to describe individual instances of language use, as distinct from LANGUE.

PASSIVE VOICE
See ACTIVE VOICE.

PERFORMANCE
A term used by Chomsky to describe a speaker's actual language use. See COMPETENCE.

PERLOCUTION
The effect of a speaker's words on hearers, such as to threaten or humour them.

PHATIC COMMUNION
Language used to establish and maintain social relations.

PHONEMES
The smallest unit of sound in a language. In Phonics, it is assumed that there are approximately 44 phonemes in English. Phonemes can be one or more letters.

PHONETICS
The study of the sounds of speech, of how sound is made, transmitted and received.

PHONICS
An approach to the teaching of reading which emphasises the sounds of words

PHONOLOGY
The study of the sounds of a particular language.

PHRASE
A part of a sentence, smaller than a clause, usually containing a headword and other modifiers.

PLOSIVES
A sound made by restricting the airflow completely and then letting the air out. Also called a stop consonant.

PRAGMATICS
The study of how people use language, their intentions, presuppositions and effects in interaction.

PREFERRED/DISPREFERRED RESPONSE
In conversational analysis, the expected response to an initiator/the response which is not expected.

PREFIX
An affix put at the front of a root word to make a new word, as in **un**dress.

PREPOSITION
Grammatical words which relate two parts of a sentence, usually in terms of physical or temporal relationships, as in *under the table* or *at lunch time*.

PRO-FORM
A linguistic item which stands in for another one, such as pronouns substituting for nouns.

PRONOUN
A word which can replace a noun: for example, personal pronouns: *he, him*; possessive pronouns: *his*; reflexive pronouns: *himself*; other categories of pronoun include relative pronouns (*which, that* etc.) and interrogative pronouns (*why, what* etc.).

PROPER NOUN
A category of noun used for individual names, places, publications, etc.

PSYCHOLINGUISTICS
The study of the relation of linguistic behaviour to mental and cognitive processes.

RECEIVED PRONUNCIATION (RP)
An English accent which has prestige. It is a social, rather than regional accent and is associated with dominant discourses such as education.

RECOUNT
The name given to a type of writing which is expository, chronological and which recounts an event or situation.

REDUNDANCY
Where utterances contain more information than is actually necessary to be understood.

REFERENCE
In cohesion, the relationship between two grammatical items.

REGISTER
The particular form of language used in a particular context and for a particular function. The concept that the form of the language is socially determined.

REPORT
The name given to a type of writing which is expository, non-chronological and which describes and explains processes.

RHEME
In a sentence, information which follows the theme, or initial indication of what the sentence is about. It tells us more about the topic of the sentence.

RHOTIC/RHOTICITY
The pronunciation, in some accents, of the *r* sound, as in *car.*

RIME
In Phonics, the part of a syllable which contains the vowel and final consonant, such as *ad* in *mad.*

SCHWA
See NEUTRAL VOWEL.

SEGMENT
In Phonics, the breaking down of a word into its constituent phonemes, such a c-a-r, c-u-p.

SEMANTICS
The study of the meanings of words.

SENTENCE
A structure containing at least a subject and a verb. Simple sentences consist of one clause, complex sentences more than one clause.

SIMILE
An expression that makes a direct and explicit comparison, usually using the words *as* or *like*.

SOCIOLECT
A dialect which is used by social, as distinct from regional, groups.

SOCIOLINGUISTICS
The study of language in a social context.

SPEECH ACTS
Utterances which perform certain functions or actions, for example, warning or requesting.

STANDARD ENGLISH
A variety of English for which a simple definition is inadequate. It exists in spoken and written form. The written standard is less controversial than the spoken standard. Spoken Standard English is the form used widely in public discourse, including education, formal settings such as the law and in broadcasting. It is the variety taught to students of English as a foreign or other language.

STOP CONSONANTS
See PLOSIVES.

SUBJECT
The subject has a direct relation to the verb, as in **be** *closed the door.*

SUBSTITUTION
In cohesion, the replacement of one form by another.

SUFFIX
An affix put at the end of a root word to change its meaning, as in *rest**ful***.

SUPERLATIVE
The form of the adjective or adverb which makes an extreme comparison, as in *biggest* or *fastest*. It can also be expressed using *most*, as in *most appropriate*.

SURFACE STRUCTURE
See DEEP STRUCTURE.

SYNONYM
A word which means the same as another word.

SYNTAX
The structural relations of words and parts of words.

TENOR
The relationship of participants in any communication, such as their relative status, roles etc.

TENSE
In grammar, the time indicated, usually by a verb, such as past, present, future.

THEME
The beginning of a sentence which gives the orientation in relation to what is being talked about.

TRANSFORMATIONAL GENERATIVE GRAMMAR
A grammar based on the system of rules underlying the structure of sentences and which, through transformations, can generate all possible forms.

TRIPHTHONGS
A sound which combines three distinct sounds.

TURN-TAKING
In discourse and conversational analysis, the way participants manage the conversation – for example, the means by which they orchestrate turns, avoid overlap, effect transitions from one speaker to another.

VELAR NASAL
The sound produced when the uvula at the back of the throat is closed, making the sound come through the nose, as in the *ing* sound when it is soft, such as in *bring.*

VOICED/UNVOICED
When a consonantal sound is made by the vibration of the vocal chords it is called voiced: without vibration it is called unvoiced. An example would be the distinction between the pronunciation of *fleas* and *fleace*.

VOWEL GLIDES
The movement in the voice between one vowel sound and another.

Children's literature

Burglar Bill, Janet and Allan Ahlberg (Heinemann 1977)
Five Go To Camp, Enid Blyton (Hodder and Stoughton 1948)
Hansel and Gretel, Anthony Browne (Little Mammoth 1981)
A Walk In The Park, Anthony Browne (Hamish Hamilton 1977)
The Midnight Fox, Betsy Byars (Heinemann 1968)
George's Marvellous Medicine, Roald Dahl (Heinemann 1981)
Revolting Rhymes, Roald Dahl (Picture Puffins 1984)
A Mouse in my Roof, Richard Edwards (Julia Macrae 1993)
The Little Boat, Kathy Henderson (Walker Books 1995)
How Tom Beat Captain Najork And His Hired Sportsmen, Russell Hoban (Jonathan Cape 1974)
Who's A Clever Girl Then? Rose Impey (Heinemann 1985)
Clever Gretchen and Other Forgotten Folktales, Alison Lurie (Mammoth 1980)
Lady Muck, William Mayne (Heinemann 1999)
Sky in the Pie, Roger McGough (Puffin 1983)
Jolly Roger and the Pirates of Abdul the Skinhead, Colin McNaughton (Walker Books 1998)
The Paperbag Princess, Robert N. Munsch (Hippo 1980)
Classic Fairy Tales, Iona and Peter Opie (Oxford University Press 1974)
The Battle Of Bubble And Squeak, Philippa Pearce (Puffin 1978)
Nightmares, Jack Prelutsky (A & C Black 1976)
The Stinky Cheese Man, Jon Scieszka and Lane Smith (Puffin 1992)
Mother Goose Goes To Cable Street, Rosemary Stones and Andrew Mann (Puffin 1980)
Catch It If You Can, edited by Brian Thompson Viking (Kestrel 1989)
Grimm's Fairy Tales, Retold by Annabel Williams-Ellis (Piccolo 1974)
Dr Xargle's Book of Earthhounds, Jeanne Willis (Andersen Press 1989)
The Singing Tortoise And Other Animal Folk Tales, Retold by John Yeoman (Gollancz 1993)

References

Austin, J. L. (1962) *How to Do Things With Words*. Oxford: Oxford University Press.

Barrs, M. (1995) 'Genre theory: what's it all about?' In B. Stierer and J. Maybin (eds) *Language, Literacy and Learning in Education*. Clevedon: Multilingual Matters.

Bartlett, R. and Fogg, D. (1992) 'Language in the environment'. In Bain, R. *et al.* (eds) *Looking into Language*. London: Hodder and Stoughton.

Bloomfield, L. (1935) *Language*. London: Allen and Unwin.

Bruner, J. S. (1985) 'Vygotsky: a historical and conceptual perspective'. In Wertsch, J. V. (ed.) *Culture, Communication and Cognition: Vygotskian Perspectives*. Cambridge: Cambridge University Press.

Cambourne, B. and Brown, H. (1989) 'Learning to control different written registers'. In Andrews, R. (ed.) *Narrative and Argument*. Milton Keynes: Open University Press.

Cameron, D. (1985) *Feminism and Linguistic Theory*. London: MacMillan.

Cameron, D. (1995) *Verbal Hygiene*. London: Routledge.

Carter, R. and Nash, W. (1990) *Seeing Through Language*. Oxford: Blackwell.

Chomsky, N. (1957) *Syntactic Structures*, The Hague: Mouton.

Chomsky, N. (1965) *Aspects of the Theory of Syntax*. MA: MIT Press.

Clarkson, G. and Stansfield, H. (1992) 'Writing recipes'. In Bain, R. *et al.* (eds) *Looking into Language*. London: Hodder and Stoughton.

Coates, J. (1989) 'Gossip revisited: language in all-female groups'. In Coates, J. and Cameron, D. *Women in their Speech Communities*. London: Longman.

Cordon, R. (2000) *Literacy and Learning Through Talk*. Buckingham: Open University Press.

Costidell, L. and Lewis, P. (2000) 'Putting Non-Fiction in the Frame', in *The Primary English Magazine*, **5**(3).

Cox, B. (1991) *Cox on Cox*. London: Hodder and Stoughton.

Crinson, J. (1997) 'Step by Step Grammar', in *The Primary English Magazine*, March/April.

Crowley, T. (1991) *Proper English*. London: Routledge.

DES (1975) *A Language for Life*. (The Bullock Report) London: HMSO.

DES (1988) *Report of the Committee of Inquiry into the Teaching of English Language*. (The Kingman Report) London: HMSO.

DES (1989) *English for Ages 5–16*. (The Cox Report) London: DES.

DfEE (1998) *The National Literacy Strategy Framework for Teaching*. London: HMSO.

Edwards, D. and Mercer, N. (1987) *Common Knowledge: The Development of Understanding in the Classroom*. London: Methuen.

Gentry, R. (1982) 'Learning to spell developmentally'. In *Reading Teacher*, **34**(4), 378–81.

Giles, H. (1971) 'Our reactions to accent'. In Mayor, B. and Pugh, A. K. (eds) (1987) *Language, Communication and Education*. London: Croom Helm.

Grice, H. P. (1975) 'Logic and conversation'. In Cole, P. and Morgan, J. L. (eds) *Syntax and Semantics 3: Speech Acts*. New York: Academic Press.

Halliday, M. A. K. (1978) *Language as a Social Semiotic*. London: Edward Arnold.

Halliday, M. A. K. (1985) *Spoken and Written Language*. Oxford: Oxford University Press.

Halliday, M.A.K. and Hasan, R. (1985) *Language, Context and Text: Aspects of Language in a Social-Semiotic Perspective*. Oxford: Oxford University Press.

Harris, R. (1962) An experimental enquiry into the functions and value of formal grammar teaching in the teaching of English. Unpublished PhD thesis, University of London.

Harris, R. and Taylor, T. (1980) *Landmarks in Linguistic Thought*. London: Routledge.

HMI (1984) *English 5–16*. London: HMSO.

HMI (1989) *Reading Policy and Practice at Ages 5–14*. London: DES.

HMSO (1921) *The Teaching of English in England*. (The Newbolt Report) London: HMSO.

Hudson, R. (2000) *Grammar Teaching and Writing skills: The Research Evidence*. http://www.phon.ucl.ac.uk/home/dick/writing.htm/

Jackson, H. (1988) *Words and Their Meanings*. London: Longman.

Johnson, S. (1747) *A Plan of a Dictionary of the English Language*. London.

Jones, N. (1990) 'Reader, writer, text'. In Carter, R. (ed.) *Knowledge about Language and the Curriculum*. London: Hodder and Stoughton.

Kress, G. (1982) *Learning to Write*. London: Routledge and Kegan Paul.

Lakoff, G. and Johnson, M. (1980) *Metaphors We Live By*. Chicago: University of Chicago Press.

Lakoff, R. (1973) *The Logic of Politeness*. Chicago: Chicago Linguistic Society.

Leech, G. N. (1983) *Principles of Pragmatics*. London: Longman.

Lewis, M. and Wray, D. (1995) *Developing Children's Non-Fiction Writing*. Leamington Spa: Scholastic.

Macauley, W. (1947) 'The difficulty of grammar'. In *British Journal of Educational Psychology*, **17**, 153–62.

McKinnon, D. (1996) 'Good and bad English', in Graddol, D. *et al.* (eds) *English: History, Diversity and Change*. London: Routledge.

Martin, J. R., *et al.* (1987) 'Social processes in education: a reply to Sawyer and Watson (and others)'. In Reid, I. (ed.) *The Place of Genre in Learning: Current Debates*. Deakin: Deakin University.

Meek, M. (1988) *How Texts Teach What Readers Learn*. Stroud: Thimble Press.

Mercer, N. (1995) *The Guided Construction of Knowledge*. Clevedon: Multilingual Matters.

Milroy, J. and Milroy, L. (1985) *Authority in Language*. London: Routledge and Kegan Paul.

Mittens, B. (1985) *English: Not the Naming of Parts*. Northants: NATE.

National Advisory Committee on Creativity and Culture (1999) *All Our Futures*. London: DfEE.

Olsen, D. R. (1984) "See! Jumping!" some oral antecedents of literacy'. In Goelman, H, *et al.* (eds) *Awakening to Literacy*. Victoria BC: University of Victoria.

Perera, K. (1984) *Children's Writing and Reading*. Oxford: Blackwell.

Perera, K. (1990) 'Grammatical differentiation between speech and writing in children aged 8 to 12'. in Carter, R. (ed.) *Knowledge about Language and the Curriculum*. London: Hodder and Stoughton.

Prentice, M. (1991) 'A Community of Enquiry', in *Talk and Learning: An In-service Pack on Oracy for Teachers*. Milton Keynes: Open University.

Priestley, J. (1761) *The Rudiments of English Grammar*. London.

Propp, V. (1928, trans. 1968) *The Morphology of the Folktale*. Austin: University of Texas Press.

Richmond, J. (1990) 'What do we mean by knowledge about language?' in Carter, R. (ed.) *Knowledge about Language and the Curriculum*. London: Hodder and Stoughton.

Riley, J. and Reedy, D. (2000) *Developing Writing for Different Purposes*. London: Chapman.

Sapir, E. (1921) *Language*. New York: Harcourt Brace and World.

de Saussure, F. (1974) *Course in General Linguistics*. London: Fontana-Collins.

Searle, J. R. (1969) *Speech Acts: An Essay in the Philosophy of Language*. Cambridge: Cambridge University Press.

Sinclair, J. and Coulthard, R. (1975) *Towards an Analysis of Discourse*. London: Oxford University Press.

Smith, F. (1992) 'Watch with mother, or view with mum?'. In Bain, R. *et al.* (eds) *Looking into Language*. London: Hodder and Stoughton.

Street, B. (1994) 'Cross-cultural Perspectives on Literacy'. In Maybin, J. (ed.) *Language and Literacy in Social Practice*. Clevedon: Multi-Lingual Matters.

Swift, J. (1712) *A Proposal for Correcting, Improving and Ascertaining the English Language*. London: Benjamin Tooke.

Thomas, J. (1995) *Meaning in Interaction*. London: Longman.

Tomlinson, D. (1994) 'Errors in the research into the effectiveness of grammar teaching'. In *English in Education*, **28**(1).

Toolan, M. (1988) *Narrative: A Critical Linguistic Introduction*. London: Routledge.

Wells, G. (1986) *The Meaning Makers*. London: Hodder and Stoughton.

Wood, G., *et al.* (1976) 'The role of tutoring in problem solving'. *Journal of Child Psychology and Psychiatry*, **17**, 89–100.

Index

Printed in the United Kingdom
by Lightning Source UK Ltd.
116313UKS00001B/487-498

9 781853 466670